FIT FOR
DISRUPTION

Published by Grammar Factory Publishing, an imprint of MacMillan Company Limited.

Grammar Factory Publishing
MacMillan Company Limited
25 Telegram Mews, 39th Floor, Suite 3906
Toronto, Ontario, Canada
M5V 3Z1

www.grammarfactory.com

Webber, Matthew, 1976
    Fit for Disruption: How to transform your business and thrive in times of rapid change / Matthew Webber.

Includes index.
ISBN: 978-1-989737-04-0

1. BUS071000 Business & Economics / Leadership. 2. BUS041000 Business & Economics / Management. 3. BUS063000 Business & Economics / Strategic Planning.

Production Credits
Printed by McPherson's Printing
Cover design by Designerbility
Interior layout design by Dania Zafar
Book production and editorial services by Grammar Factory Publishing

FIT FOR
DISRUPTION

HOW TO TRANSFORM YOUR BUSINESS AND THRIVE IN TIMES OF RAPID CHANGE

MATTHEW WEBBER

CONTENTS

DEDICATION AND ACKNOWLEDGEMENTS

I would like to dedicate this book to Kelly: my best friend and the beautiful soul I married. I thank you for the love and support that you provide unconditionally. I thank you for and deeply respect your professional counsel and your significant contribution to this book. Above all I thank you for your unwavering belief in me, and for every moment that you have helped me believe in myself. Without you, this book simply would not be. Nor would the next one.

A massive thank you also to those who helped produce this book, and who have taken the time to provide advice and review – Simon Murphy, Adam Noakes, Nicholas Canavan and, of course, Kelly. Nicholas, I thank you also for preparing me for this journey.

To Scott, Carolyn and the team at Grammar Factory – your remarkable support and guidance made this possible. From the concept design, editing (which was no small feat), cover design, even the name of the book – your value is immeasurable, and I cannot thank you enough for helping turn this book into what it is, which is something I am incredibly proud of. I thank also Caroline Czajkowski and Caza Creative for the illustration work that supported bringing the 'Fit for Disruption' concepts to life.

A special mention to my children: Rhylee, Abbey, Noah and Emmerson. Keep dreaming BIG and believing anything is possible. Keep your minds open and be kind always. Do what you love and love what you do – the rest will fall into place. This book is but one example.

INTRODUCTION

KODAK INVENTED THE DIGITAL CAMERA IN 1975. AND YET THEY chose not to develop the technology and continued to rely on profits made by selling film. After all, they thought, they were in the film business – why would they promote competitive technology that would threaten their bottom line? The answer, of course, was because if they didn't start selling digital cameras, another company would. Which is precisely what happened, and what put Kodak out of business. The fact that the camera was a digital device meant that new players could enter the market and the distribution strength of Kodak was weakened. While 1975 may have been a little early for the new technology, by the time Kodak realised they needed to act on the innovation, it was too late. They held on to outdated assumptions for too long. They failed to see that the world had shifted and there were new paradigms being created.

Kodak isn't the only example of what, in hindsight, were obviously huge corporate blunders. For example, would you believe that Blockbuster had the opportunity to buy Netflix?

But you don't have to be the next Kodak, or the next Blockbuster. Disruption can kill companies, but the smart ones can find opportunities in disruptive times. Airbnb was founded in 2008. The business was launched at the height of the global financial crisis, and Airbnb provided a way to minimise costs for travellers and also allow homeowners to generate extra income that was needed in tough times. If the concept had been launched years earlier, homeowners might not have had the motivation, or necessity, to come on board. The financial crisis provided the impetus for people to relax their perceptions and have an open mind to new alternatives. Airbnb is now valued at over $20 billion and is in thousands of cities around the world. It competes with the largest of all the hotel chains without owning a single property.

Uber is another example of an innovation that capitalised on disruption. It arrived at a time when people were looking for better value in personal transport. Taxis had become very expensive, and had a bad reputation for cleanliness, comfort and service standards. The uptake of smartphones was peaking at the same time, and convenience was one of the highest priorities for a busy world. Then there was the idle capacity of private vehicles – think of how often you drive down a freeway and see a car with just one person in it – and people saw this as an opportunity to make extra money during difficult times. But Uber was just the start. There is now an entire shared economy being created out of excess capacity – people are on-selling space in their homes (Airbnb), space in restaurants outside trading hours for coworking space (Kettlespace) and even unused personal caravans (Camplify).

Whom would you rather be? Kodak or Airbnb? Blockbuster or Uber?

Each of these companies either capitalised on change or was a victim of change. Today, the world is changing more rapidly than ever, and businesses are becoming more and more likely to be affected by disruption. But remember, disruption also brings opportunity. We don't know what that opportunity will be, but you don't need to know – you just need to be change-ready and learn how to make a profit in a disruptive environment.

A CHANGING WORLD

The world we know has changed. The speed, the relationships, the priorities, the tastes. We can access information, goods and services quicker than ever. Companies and governments know more than ever about our behaviours, our habits, our movements, our relationships and our histories.

The way we communicate with each other has changed enormously; we spend less time at the dinner table and more time swiping up, down, left and right for news and updates on our social groups, or even to find a new life partner. We are living in a world that is more connected than ever.

The world has become smaller as travel has become more accessible and affordable, and trade between countries from all corners of the globe has opened. But the political environment is volatile, and we are seeing China and Asia re-emerge in political, social and economic contexts.

We have ageing populations that will create significant challenges very soon. The younger generation is desperate for us to actively tackle the global climate challenge.

It sounds like the world has gone crazy, but the reality is that the world has always been changing. In fact, we are conditioned for change – we have always needed it for our survival. Things do not stay the same; we are forever evolving and developing and today, right now, we are in one of the most dynamic periods of change that has ever been seen. Forget the Industrial Revolution; now we are facing the Digital Revolution, and this change is happening at a much, much faster rate.

The good news is that this rapid change is throwing up an endless supply of opportunity. But organisations need to be adaptable to be able to grasp this opportunity. They need to be able to move with lightning speed and they need to be awake and ready. To be ready we must first understand the environment we are in. It is disruptive. It requires different thinking – creative thinking.

The opportunity is now, right this very second.

To make the most of this opportunity, let's consider the different ways the world is changing, and how this is likely to affect your business.

Digitisation

The Digital Age is upon us right now. It is the new economy. This era is re-shaping every aspect of our social, economic and political environment, and we are now all dependent upon information and technology to function. Many people fear this technological dominance in our lives. As with any new currency, there is always a chance that it will be misused or used for evil. However, if we start with a premise that this digital era is evil, we will miss all the great opportunity that it has to help society progress and to make this world a happier, healthier place.

The application of digital and data capability will lead to far greater opportunities for organisations to prosper, if they can manage it wisely. This is because digital and data allows for greater connectivity and the ability to manage enormous amounts of information. It enables more opportunities for collaboration by sharing information and reducing duplication of effort. Organisations that can use digital and data to create meaningful insights, and to develop greater efficiencies in their operations, will be well positioned to drive better business performance and profit.

Globalisation

The world has opened up and now has an infinite amount of opportunity. Digitisation and cheaper air travel have made business accessible to more people across the globe. A fifteen-year-old from Australia can buy and sell goods made in China, India and the US from the comfort of her bedroom. Communities in Africa can access micro loans from European countries to start entrepreneurial ventures to lift them out of poverty. A clothing retailer can be on the catwalk in Paris researching the newest fashion one day, be in China the next developing designs, and have the product in store in multiple countries just weeks later.

Retailers can now source products from countries with lower production costs; a law firm can operate in many international jurisdictions; travel companies can accommodate the influx and outflux of business and leisure travellers; global businesses can be operated from home. Even the freelance economy has boomed, allowing a graphic designer in the Philippines to do marketing work for a company in the US, or a copywriter in the UK to work for someone in New Zealand. A Pho restaurant in Vietnam is in competition with multinational fast food giants like KFC and McDonalds.

The onset of technological advancement, and the maturity of cultural and economic understanding between countries, has made this possible. New players have emerged, as have stronger ones. Big companies, small companies and individual entrepreneurs can all operate on the global stage – all they need is a smartphone or a laptop and access to the internet.

This all means that we face greater competition from foreign firms, and from a disaggregated supply base such as entrepreneurs and small, nimble businesses. The fact is, if you are not prepared to operate in a global setting, it is unlikely that you will survive.

The twenty-first century is expected to be the century of Asia – when the region, led by China, will start to dominate the economic and political agenda of the world. The East has a very different perspective from the West on many issues, and this in itself will change business and social behaviour at a global level. The region is densely populated and is emerging in terms of wealth and capability. It is, in fact, becoming the growth engine of the world.

The 'now' economy

We are living in a world that is accessible, and where time is poor and options are plentiful.

We want information in real time. We want our food delivered to our door. When I was studying for my high school exams, I had to make an hour-long bus trip to go to the library and search catalogues in the hope of finding a valuable reference resource. Now my children just Google anything they need to learn.

We can watch a movie, a television show or even a sporting event at any time. Now people watch entertainment on mobile devices, and if they miss what they wanted to watch they don't need to have to set a recorder. It is all available on demand.

It is a 'now' economy; it is fast, and it is furious.

The customer-driven economy

One thing is for sure, with more information and more options on the market, with such quick response times and the ability to broadcast customer satisfaction levels to any part of the globe in an instant, the control of the economy sits with the customer. The customer is expecting you to come to them with new ideas, insights and methods, and develop products that will delight them. They are turning to you because they want that freshness. The customer will now be able to tell you what they want, and in fact are more willing than ever before to work with you on getting what they want right.

We don't want to be the same as everyone else; we want our needs to be serviced as and when they arise. We want everything customised for us. Customisation or personalisation is becoming more important to the customer. While you don't want to try to be all things to all people, you should build into your business model a way of providing a personalised experience – one that empathises with the customer and understands what their problems are.

But customers are not just buyers; they can also be your advocates – or your nemesis. Customers have always had power, but the tidal wave of social media means that your customers can broadcast their make or break opinions about your business to vast global audiences, almost effortlessly. Your company is on 24/7 watch.

The new generation gap

A decade or two ago, it seemed that the generation gap was dead. Parents and their children listened to the same music, went to the same movies, and even borrowed each other's clothes. But now the generation gap is back with a vengeance, and the difference between Millennials and their formerly 'switched on' parents is having an impact.

It will be the younger generation that will shape the economy and how it is conducted. They will be the ones doing the work, and they have been educated in a time when technology has been the norm. They have work methods available to them that older generations could never have imagined, and their priorities are different.

Equally we cannot ignore the contribution that more mature generations can make. Wise counsel and support will be required for the younger generations as they embark on this fast and furious transition into a digital and global economy. There are also issues and opportunities that arise from an ageing population. Health care is a growth area, but there is also a loss of skills and knowledge as a large part of the workforce enters retirement.

Some commentators count as many as five generations within the workforce, and the differences between the generations are not subtle. The adaptability to digitisation, globalisation and even environmental and political challenges is vastly different. Social norms, education, availability of resources and even just expectations will differ greatly. However, this diversity and difference offers an incredible opportunity for creative and innovative thinking.

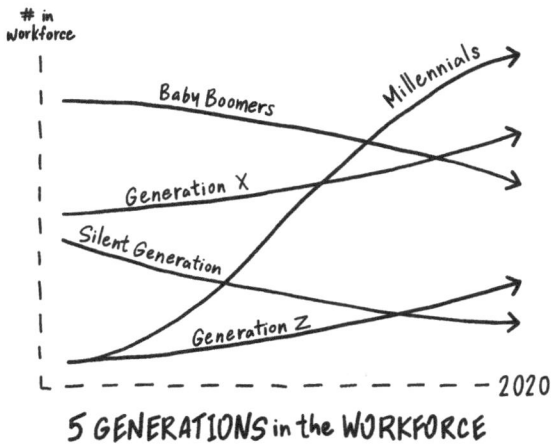

5 GENERATIONS in the WORKFORCE

Gig, contract and flexible work

The way that we work now is changing. The idea of traditional employment relationships is fast becoming redundant.

The 'gig' economy is becoming increasingly popular as employment relationships are conducted on a needs basis. Independent workers are contracted for fixed-term appointments or on a needs basis to fulfil a specific purpose at a specific moment.

Corporate structures, legal frameworks and even services required to facilitate the gig economy will need to be developed to accommodate this emerging trend. New tools, services and platforms will have to be created to support this new way of working. It is becoming widely accepted now that with all the new digital capabilities, along with a very global economy, flexibility can be incorporated into employment relationships. Work, in most cases, can be performed anywhere at any time and all that is needed is the right equipment, such as a laptop and smart phone and access to high-speed internet. Even where workers don't join the gig economy, and stick with more traditional employment relationships, there will be demand for flexible working conditions and arrangements.

So, if the world is changing so quickly, and in so many different and *unpredictable* ways, how can a business get ready for that change? Surely it's impossible in this disruptive environment. Well, I'm here to tell you that it's not impossible. That if you apply a few key principles in your business, you will position yourself to capitalise on these changes rather than collapse under their weight.

GET READY TO DO BUSINESS DIFFERENTLY

Ultimately, it comes down to the way that an organisation sees itself, and whether it has an embedded culture of improvement or one of complacency and maintaining the status quo.

Be ready

Internally, a company must be ready. Capacity, time, resources and capabilities are required, and if they are already depleted or exhausted it will make surviving a disruption more difficult.

Organisations that work *on* the business are far more likely to make the organisation ready and able to take the next step. Those organisations focused on working *in* the business will be so focused on operations and dealing with current problems and resource constraints that it will be difficult for them to be ready to improve at the level and pace that is required to succeed in today's environment.

We don't know what disruptions are in front of us, and the further out that those disruptions are the less likely it is that we can predict them and determine how to manage them. However, you will have a much better outcome if you can control how events play out. Being prepared will give you the best chance of being able to do that. There will be greater resource lost and wasted by reacting than by preparing. It is about having the relationships, supply chain and systems in place that can respond with agility and conviction.

Develop your innovation muscles

Developing a culture in your business that focuses on innovation and improvement is not an easy task; it requires patience and resilience. However, you need to exercise your innovation and business improvement muscles, and you need to nourish those muscles over time so that they can perform when you need them most.

Being persistent, and training the innovation and business improvement muscles, even when it is hardest, gives you the strength to take on the new business environment and be able to react swiftly to most circumstances. If you have not exercised these muscles, you will be slow to respond, you will run out of breath and you will risk other unintended consequences because you have not prepared yourself adequately or appropriately.

Lose the fear of failure

'I have not failed. I've just found 10,000 ways that won't work.'
THOMAS EDISON

Fear is a natural part of the human condition. It has helped us to survive. If we didn't fear lions, we wouldn't have run away from them. There is no prize for being caught by a lion.

But we are no longer being chased by lions and tigers; now we live in a world where we don't have to win at every situation. We can place our fears into context. If we didn't, we would probably stay at home all day every day and never cross the street again.

Think of the price of not trying because you were paralysed by fear. The biggest disappointments in life are not our failures, but rather our regrets that chances were not taken. People on their deathbeds don't dwell on their failures; they are more likely to be cursing not having taken the opportunities they had.

But some people have the courage to seize opportunities. Jeff Bezos left a secure career to found Amazon; Steve Jobs dropped out of college; Elon Musk has probably crashed more rockets than he would care to remember. They have become great because of the chances they have taken, the fear they placed into context and the drive they had to leave a legacy.

Obviously, you don't want to be reckless, and you should understand your own limitations and those of others. But don't be afraid of failure; just make sure you fail the right way.

Have the right mindset

Can you imagine the risk of failure when John F Kennedy ('JFK') said, on May 25, 1961, that America would put a man on the moon before the end of the decade? The science and engineering capability to do that did not exist when he made this statement, yet there was an unwavering belief it could and would be done. And we have just passed the fiftieth anniversary of man taking those first steps on the moon. JFK believed without proof. The business of innovation and continuous improvement needs a positive mindset. Having people who can look to reasons why you can, rather than why you cannot, sets the base by which great innovations can succeed. There is often a tendency to over-analyse ideas and proposals, which leads to inaction. But having a positive mindset enables people not to be overwhelmed by problems, and instead see the opportunities within them, and work with others to find effective and meaningful solutions that create value.

Be ethical

To be ethical is to do the right thing. Some of the challenges you may face include working in emerging countries where bribery, corruption and child labour are rampant. Digitisation creates challenges around the collection, storage and use of customer and personal data. You may have to decide whether you're willing to use genetically modified ingredients in your food products. While many of these ethical challenges will not be new, they will become magnified in a disruptive environment and exposure to them will increase exponentially. But they can be your friend.

Your customers are increasingly expecting you and your organisation to act in an ethical manner. Customers are now gravitating towards companies that are not only outwardly doing the right thing, but also actively giving back to society.

These ethical challenges spell opportunity for organisations. Not only can they meet the standards required, but a competitive advantage can be gained by operating with a purpose greater than the organisation itself. Not to mention that doing the right thing is, well, just the right thing to do.

Be adaptable

Adaptability is the ability to be flexible in new situations, handle change and balance multiple demands and stimulants. It is about 'being comfortable with the uncomfortable' and having a mindset that not only embraces rapid change but is able to thrive in that environment.

With the onset of technological advancement at an exponential rate, and with the development and shift in society, the greatest predictor of success will soon become, if it is not already, the ability to adapt – and adapt quickly. This will be true for individuals, families, teams, organisations, even governments.

We will need to be able to lead our people and organisations through these periods of rapid change. We will need sure-fire ways of quickly resolving problems, engaging people in the process and moving forward at pace without the wheels falling off. This will have to be done in a calm, collected and resilient manner.

And how do I know all these things? I have been lucky enough to work in some great, and not so great, organisations across the globe. I have been involved in some very successful operations and innovation change programs that have delivered tens (if not hundreds) of millions of dollars of benefits and impacted thousands of people for the better.

I have worked in businesses that were in crisis and haemorrhaging financially and culturally. I have helped rebuild many of these companies, and some I have had to close. One program I delivered fundamentally changed the way that over 25,000 people operated, giving meaning to their work where previously there was chaos. But what delights me most is that today I can walk into the environments where I influenced change, and the change remains obvious. The change has lasted.

Many of my insights come not from the successes (although they do help), but from the failures that I have experienced. This is where I have learned the most. It is essential to know what good looks like, but also to know what failure looks like – and *feels* like.

These opportunities have helped me identify three types of business:

- First are the organisations that have become profitable industry leaders, sometimes coming from a very unprofitable position;
- Then there are the organisations that have become unprofitable and irrelevant after being profitable industry leaders; and
- Finally, there are those that just languish in mediocrity.

I have come to understand that organisations that are highly successful and profitable industry leaders have certain attributes in common, as do those that are not.

This book attempts to unpack these attributes and share insights from the perspective of someone who has lived and breathed these environments. I have felt the pains and enjoyed the highs, and I have learned from successes and failures alike – at both leadership and operator level.

My experiences have helped me identify the attributes that are required to transform an organisation into a profitable industry leader during an era of disruption.

INTRODUCING THE FIT FOR DISRUPTION MODEL

Business leaders can lead their organisations into the future. They can embrace the disruption and change that the business world is experiencing and provide the direction and environment that helps make the most of these opportunities. To do this, it makes sense to have an approach, a mindset and a framework that helps leaders and organisations focus their efforts. The Fit for Disruption model is just such an approach and is based on the three attributes that all successful leaders and organisations possess.

- The leaders and organisations that are Fit for Disruption have a focus on the structure and control of the organisation. They understand where they are going and why they are going there, and they know how to make every dollar count. They are **Commercial**.

- Leaders and organisations that are Fit for Disruption don't stand still. They are inquisitive and they want to be better at what they do. They never reach their destination because they are always pushing the boundary forward. They love to solve problems, and to do so they engage people who are best placed to help solve problems. These leaders and organisations are innovators. They **Create** solutions.

- Leaders and organisations that are Fit for Disruption can build momentum and energy around a cause. They can take an idea and make it happen. They walk the talk and have an insatiable appetite for getting things done. They are not pontificators; they are action orientated. They embrace **Change.**

The Fit for Disruption framework is based on these three key attributes and has a simple objective – to help leaders and organisations deliver rapid profit improvement in times of disruption and uncertainty.

HOW TO USE THE MODEL

The Fit for Disruption method is a holistic approach. Each attribute has equal weight, and while you may excel in one or two of them, and as honourable as that would be, it will only support mediocrity. All attributes have to be addressed if you want to be Fit for Disruption.

For example, you may have the ability to sustain business performance through **CHANGE**; however, if you cannot change and be profitable – that is, be commercial – at the same time, your change will be either short lived or will make the business vulnerable. How many companies have entered new markets, introduced new products or started operating in new territories only to dilute profit performance?

It's also important to understand that the Fit for Disruption framework is not about perfection; it is about improvement. You are most likely to be at different maturity levels for each attribute, and while it would be nice to have each attribute perfected and functioning at an optimal level, it's important to remember that it is a journey, not a destination. As long as you start to move the dial in a positive direction on each attribute, the method will start having an impact.

The method is not linear, it is circular, and each attribute depends on each of the others. At different times organisations will have to place more or less effort on one of the attributes, or they may need to jump from one to the other depending on the situation. You just need to get started.

Fortune favours the bold. We are often hamstrung from procrastination or we get stuck in our own limited mindset and cannot move forward. Being bold is about overcoming the limitations we place on ourselves, our people and our organisations, and inspiring others to be all that we can be. Being bold is about having authenticity and confidence in your own judgement and being resourceful enough to make your dreams reality.

While your competitors and peers are stuck in a pattern of inertia, you and your organisation are taking on the new era with a refreshing sense of confidence. You are making it happen, you are living your values and you are adding immense value to everyone in your organisation's business ecosystem.

The rewards are simply too good to ignore. Not only will you avoid becoming irrelevant in your industry, you will become a gravitational centre for people who want to make a difference and who want to leave a legacy. You will have a say in how our society is shaped, and what the future of business looks like. You won't be a mere bystander having this all happening to you; you will be shaping it.

PART 1

BE COMMERCIAL

THE FIRST ATTRIBUTE IN THE FIT FOR DISRUPTION MODEL IS TO BE Commercial. This is your ability to drive accelerated business performance through structure, discipline and operational excellence. While the creative elements of business are fun, there are times we need to turn on our logical brain and ensure that we have the necessary discipline to make the most of our opportunities. Innovation can only occur with a strong commercial foundation.

Strong commercial discipline will not only ensure that valuable resources are prioritised and allocated properly, it will be the very vehicle that will help you accelerate your growth in a period of disruption. The discipline will allow you to respond with speed and certainty and, importantly, ensure that you are focused on the opportunities that will provide the greatest value.

It may seem counter-intuitive, but the enemy of creativity and innovation is poor commercial control. There is absolutely no fun in having an underperforming business and having everyone distracted by trying to resuscitate it. Being profitable gives the space and, dare I say it, structure to enable the creative process to work.

Our organisations need to be efficient and lean to prosper. Excess slows us down; it makes us unhealthy. Efficiency sets the base from which you can create; it helps everyone understand the baseline. It is like building core strength. If you can operate efficiently, you can take more on, you can pivot your focus quickly, and you can manage the tempo and have it on your terms.

If you are not profitable right now, don't despair. The objective is to get you profitable as quickly as possible so that your attentions are not divided. I have worked with many organisations that have not been profitable, but after concentrating on the fundamentals of being profitable, they have been able to turn their focus to innovation and have had a great level of success. I have also worked with organisations that have been uber-profitable but allowed complacency to set in and weak controls to emerge that have stripped away all value – to the point where they no longer exist, or have to fight for survival rather than innovate to thrive.

The key steps to being **Commercial** are:

1. Develop a **Strategy** and **Strategic Plan** – know what business you are in and why;
2. Build a **Governance Framework** that helps you maintain control as you grow;
3. Design a **Business Intelligence** capability that will provide insights, analytics, reporting and KPIs that are relevant, timely and support effective decision making; and
4. Make every dollar count by having a **Profit Improvement Program** in place.

COMMERCIAL MODEL

1. DEVELOP a STRATEGY and STRATEGIC PLAN

Know what business you are in and **WHY**

2. BUILD a GOVERNANCE FRAMEWORK that helps you maintain control

3. DESIGN a BUSINESS INTELLIGENCE CAPABILITY that will provide insights, analytics, reporting and KPIs that are relevant, timely and support effective decision making.

4. Make every dollar count by having a PROFIT IMPROVEMENT PLAN

CHAPTER 1

DEVELOP A STRATEGY

DEVELOPING A STRATEGY FOR YOUR BUSINESS IS THE FIRST STEP to being commercial. A big picture strategy should take into account the internal and external environment, along with the key considerations and steps that need to be taken to achieve an objective. It will consider overarching timeframes, risks, market conditions, and an assessment of the overall opportunity. It will consider the organisation's capacity to achieve the objectives, what gaps may be present, and ultimately how to overcome those gaps. However, before you create your strategy, you need to understand why you're in business and what business you are in. Answering these questions will help you define the objective that you set out in your strategy.

WHY ARE YOU IN BUSINESS?

Successfully articulating why you are in business is an effective way to communicate and define your value in a way that will inspire people to act. You are probably familiar with Simon Sinek's theory, which is that by communicating why you are in business you tap into the part of the listener's brain that influences behaviour. Your 'Why' becomes your differentiator and the reason customers will want to do business with you. As Sinek argues, people do not buy what you do; they buy *why* you do it.

The 'Why' will inform the big picture strategy. Once you have your Why, it becomes easier to understand what type of resources you need and how to organise your business. It will define everything, such as where you operate, the type of materials you use, whom you will partner with and the type of people you should employ. It is crucial that an organisation understands why it does what it does, so that resources and energy are not wasted on things that are not important.

Think of Lego's Why – '... *to Inspire and develop the builders of tomorrow*'

The most important aspect to the strategy, and the Why, is that it is understood and embraced by everyone in your organisation. The Why sets the direction and will centre the organisation when difficult or conflicting decisions need to be made. The Why will guide decision making and ensure that the organisation continues towards the agreed objective. It will also help to indicate when a change of course is required.

For example, you may be a health food retailer that wants to help build a world without obesity and cancer – this is why you are in business. If you forget why you are in business, you may compromise and started selling sugar lollies and soft drinks. But this would be in direct conflict with why your organisation exists, and would confuse the customers and the brand, ultimately causing you to lose credibility in the market and alienate employees.

In considering why you are in business, you also have an opportunity to create a purpose-led business. For example, eyewear company Warby Parker's Why, as stated on their website, is: *'to offer designer eyewear at a revolutionary price, while leading the way for socially conscious businesses.'*

Having a purpose such as this, powerful and clearly defined, will help guide your business in every decision that it makes. It will influence whom you hire and whom you partner with, help to define the supply chain, and support commercial imperatives such as driving sales because you know that others will benefit.

It is likely that the customer will be more loyal as they buy into your vision. This will create an emotional connection that is hard to break. A competitor may be able to offer products or services at a similar price point and quality, but if you can also connect with customers' emotional needs, you are likely to have the competitive edge.

Being purpose-led will not only attract customers to your organisation, it will also help attract and retain the right type of talent. When your employees, especially new ones, share the same values, it will be much easier to align the organisation to the strategy and to get momentum. This will help you to operate with speed and efficiency as you are not spending time getting everyone aligned.

Remember, however, that you must be authentic. Many companies purport to be values-led but are only trying to attract attention. Customers and other people will see straight through this, and it will have a lasting, damaging effect as trust will be broken.

Another great benefit of having shared values is that there are business opportunities in solving social problems. This is not about meeting social expectations around issues such as corporate responsibility, nor is it charity. It is about using the business for the benefit of all – for the common good. It is at the heart of the organisation – it defines the entire being of the organisation.

WHAT BUSINESS ARE YOU IN?

If Kodak had realised they were in the business of capturing memories, rather than the business of film, they'd have seen the opportunity that digital technology presented. If Blockbuster knew they were in the business of content distribution, not DVD hire, they might have had a fighting chance. McDonalds know they are in the space of fast food, not fine dining. Jetstar Airways know their job is to accommodate budget and holiday travellers, not business travellers.

Knowing what business you are in will help you to understand your customers' problems. Understanding what problems you are solving, and for whom, allows you to develop innovative solutions that add tangible value for your customers. People don't buy hammers; they buy the ability to hang a painting on the wall, or to construct a house, or to bend a pipe into shape. It is not about the hammer; it is about what the hammer can do and whether it can solve a problem.

How did the tobacco industry survive so long? It marketed itself not on its product, but on the lifestyle and social benefits. When Pepsi and Coca Cola are advertising, they portray an image of lifestyle. High-end designer brands like Gucci and Prada are selling social status, and if you play the lottery by buying a ticket, you are buying the dream, not the ticket.

Too many businesses fail by trying to be all things to all people and failing to focus on what they are good at and where they can add value. When I started working for a large, struggling retailer, I was confused as to why they were selling expensive designer apparel with a price point well above what the demographic would be prepared or could afford to pay. In their hard goods section, they were selling toasters for $7.00 but were trying to instil a quality image. It made no sense, and they were trying to be all things to all people. The customers were confused, and this retailer struggled in the marketplace for some time.

Conversely, another retail brand I worked for were very clear that they were operating at the value end of the market, and everything was about offering the lowest prices on everyday items. The range reflected that strategy and the customers understood and embraced the offer. This retailer won that segment convincingly, and they continue to do so, because they were very clear on whom their customer was and focused on them.

HOW WILL YOU ACHIEVE YOUR GOAL?

You will achieve your goal by adhering to your values – the values and behaviours that need to be entrenched in the culture of the organisation that support and provide substance to its purpose. In this context, the 'How' is the values and behaviours of the organisation.

Values will differ from organisation to organisation. For instance, an airline or a mining or logistics company would have safety as a core value, given the risk profile of those industries. It would be very hard to operate if that was not a core value. But for a professional services firm, such as a law practice or accounting firm, safety may not be a core value; not because they do not believe safety is important, but because their risk profile is different. Regardless of your risk profile, however, in times of disruption, I would suggest including INNOVATION as a core value. Unless you innovate, you will not be fit for disruption.

Of course, you cannot simply put a value up on a poster and assume that the organisation will adopt it. It must run deeper than that – to entrench the value, people need to believe in it and be aligned with it.

YOUR GRAND STRATEGIC PLAN

Now that we've considered the broad principles that should govern your strategy, let's look in more detail at the plans you should be making.

Strategic plans are meaningless unless they are executed and treated as a living document that everyone can understand, communicate and recite. They cannot simply be written and then placed on a shelf, or in a file on a computer never to be seen again. There needs to be structure and governance around the agreed plan and the leadership and operational teams need to be constantly reviewing the plan in both a structured format, such as monthly and quarterly reviews, as well as ad hoc reviews that occur when something happens that requires an adjustment to the plan. The plan must also be measured against performance targets. It is important to keep tracking how well you are doing so that you can adjust the tempo or direction.

The strategic plan is also used as a means of communication with internal and external stakeholders to generate buy-in and engagement in the goals of the organisation. The plan should also articulate how it affects the various stakeholders, and how its success will benefit them. Ideally, you should engage your key stakeholders in the process. It is much easier to execute a plan if stakeholders are party to developing it. They then own it, buy into it and will have a vested emotional interest in bringing it to life.

It does not matter what your starting point is; even if your business is unprofitable, you still need to write a plan and set a direction. Being unprofitable just means you have not yet figured out how to be profitable, which is why you need the Fit for Disruption model to help you understand how to drive profit from your organisational efforts.

Now let's take a look at the main elements of a strategic plan.

Aspirations, goals and objectives

To this point we have been discussing the Why, What and How of the business strategy. In other words, the broad principles that should guide you. You may now be looking to ground the strategy into practical components that lead to actions. From this point the elements of a good strategy will take on a more practical and tangible flavour and provide concrete direction to inform the organisation of the activities and considerations it must undertake in order to create a reality. This is where the strategy needs to paint a very clear picture of where the organisation is going and what it wants to achieve. The more specific, the better.

Aspirations and goals can be expressed in financial terms, such as:

- 20% sales growth
- 5% profit growth
- 15% return on capital

You can then turn these numbers into an objective statement. For example, if we were writing a strategy for an imaginary airline, it could be:

Lowest price, economy air travel, for holiday makers.

This statement is clear and concise; there is no ambiguity. Look at the first two words of the statement: 'lowest price' – it is clear they will compete on price and will need to design their whole business around being able to invest in price as a competitive advantage. It identifies the market position the airline is going for and, no surprises, it is at the budget end of the market. It uses the words *economy air travel*. It clearly does not mean car hire or hotel bookings. Nor does it mean that the airline offers business class. It says it there in black and white – they are in the business of economy air travel.

Then there is a reference to holiday makers. It again is clear – they are not chasing business travellers, or anyone flying for a purpose other than holidays. Now, of course, this does not mean that business travellers *won't* fly with the airline – in fact, they probably will – but the point is that the organisation is not focusing on them; it is focused on their efforts in their niche and core market.

Operational tactics

The strategy must articulate the operational tactics the company will deploy in order to achieve its objectives. Items that will be considered here can include, but are not limited to:

- The five Ps – Product, People, Price, Promotion, Place;
- Focus markets, customers and geographies;
- Supply chain alignment;
- Technology alignment;
- Organisation of resources, including people;
- Assets that need to be deployed;
- A timeline, and understanding of key milestones;
- Key dependencies;
- Key risks and mitigations;
- Alignment of accountabilities; and
- Communication principles.

The level of detail required in this section will obviously depend on the level of the strategy and the time span. Generally speaking, strategies have a span between three and five years, while there will be periodic spans, such as annual plans, which need to tie up to the overall strategy.

One thing is certain, and that is that the business environment will change continuously, and whatever assumptions you make today about tomorrow will almost invariably be wrong. The longer the time span, the greater the gap between expectation and reality. However, this is not to say that you cannot have a long-range vision. The trick is to keep it focused enough to provide direction, but adaptable enough to be able to change the way you solve the problem it addresses. For example, Kodak could have created a strategy to focus on film in the twentieth century and digital technology in the twenty-first century, while accepting that even digital technology will eventually become obsolete.

It is important that you align your shorter-term activities, efforts and resource allocation (such as monthly, quarterly and annual cycles) with the master strategy – remembering that the master strategy is an intent and ambition, not a fixed course of action and destination. By definition, the master strategy will have less detail than a short-range plan, but it is crucial that the two are aligned.

Finance, measurement and funding

Finally, the strategy should consider and address the fundamental financial and commercial aspects of your business. The numbers don't necessarily have to be elaborate, but they do need to guide you and provide an anchor point for your targets. Points to include are:

- Key forecasts – What are the projected impacts on cashflow and P&L, and when will they occur?
- Capital allocation – Where will capital be deployed and when?
- Governance and reporting – How will you monitor performance against the objectives and timelines of the strategy, and what controls will be in place to ensure transparency and alignment?
- Assumptions – What are the key assumptions, both financial and non-financial, of the strategy?
- Funding – How will the strategy be funded?

A strategy cannot be a set and forget exercise. It needs to be lived and breathed by your entire organisation, and, most importantly, it needs to be understood by the people who need to take action.

FIRST THINGS FIRST

Now we have spent time on developing a strategy, which will provide the overall business direction and clarity that must manifest into meaningful action. We have considered the Why, What and How, and have covered operational tactics, finance, commercial and funding. But there's more...

I'd like you to consider an additional element in the development of your strategy. It's what I call the Moonshot Maturity Model. I want to bring particular attention to this model because it will be your secret weapon in a disruptive environment, where we can either be disrupted or can play the game on our terms and become the disrupter.

The Moonshot Maturity Model provides a blank slate that allows your organisation to ask: 'What if?' Legacies are built on aspiration, and this model provides a framework to be able to articulate the aspiration. The beauty of this model is that you can overlay your business strategy with it. It should be noted, however, that while the Why, What and How of your strategy will be consistent, the elements of aspirational goals and objectives, operational tactics, and finance, management and funding would need to be modified for each step in the Moonshot Maturity Model.

While we do advocate innovating and being prepared to cannibalise redundant products or businesses, we also recognise that we often still need to protect the golden goose. We must protect value that remains in the business, and we must transition carefully.

The model is progressive and builds upon itself. I'll use Qantas as an example to illustrate each step.

1. The basics

This is about reviewing your current operations. It sounds self-explanatory, but you should look at everything you are doing in your business and sit down to review whether it's aligned with your Why. If something is not connected to your Why, stop doing it. If it doesn't support the end game, stop doing it or at least adjust.

There is no point trying to be operationally excellent or grow your business unless you have your foundations right. It is quite alarming to see an organisation trying to be very clever and implement new ways of doing business when the business that they already have has plenty of value still waiting to be extracted, or when they simply can't get the basics right, such as paying employees or suppliers on time.

Qantas example:
- Making profit from existing routes
- Improving on-time departure rates
- Refining aircraft maintenance schedule

2. Core excellence

At this stage you aim to be the very best at what you do and extract maximum value from your investment. Achieving core excellence means that you can execute every part of your business more efficiently than your competitors and in a way that is consistent with your strategy. It also means that you are profitable and providing a very healthy return on investment.

Qantas example:
- Upgrading fleet to most fuel-efficient planes
- Having the best airport lounges and check-in counters, including self-serve and online check-in
- Loyalty program, superior entertainments systems and onboard wi-fi

3. Growth and new business
The next phase is to identify how you can take that core excellence and apply it to new areas, such as complementary products. If you can, do this without destroying your core.

Qantas example:
- New routes into new destinations
- Starting a new airline (as they did with Jetstar as a budget carrier alternative)
- Moving into financial services and insurance products

4. BHAG (big hairy audacious goal)
Now that your business is grounded, it's time to start thinking about taking off. An organisation needs to ensure that it has sufficient stretch in its objectives. Setting a BHAG is one method to do this. It sets a tone that the organisation is prepared to believe beyond what is deemed possible from an internal and external perspective. While not impossible, the BHAG will require full alignment and effort. If the BHAG is achieved, the organisation's business performance will lift exponentially, ultimately becoming a game changer. The BHAG will be relative to the organisation and what limitations, perceived or real, it may have. A BHAG may be as simple as growing tenfold, opening in an international market or gaining a contract with a major global brand.

Qantas example:

- Non-stop flight from New York to Sydney, or from Perth to London
- Being carbon neutral
- Establishing a pilot academy to produce 500 pilots per year, with intake of female pilots to be forty per cent

5. Moonshot

The moonshot is highly ambitious, highly exploratory and may (or may not) have high degrees of complication attached to it.

Moonshots are the Airbnbs, the Facebooks, the Googles, the Ubers – the game-changing movements that have a part in history.

Qantas example (hypothetical):

- Enter space travel market and, literally, offer flights to the moon!!!

Of course, I'm exaggerating here – but why not? I'm encouraging you to think as big as you can. But remember that a moonshot is contextual. For some, just opening a small business may be the equivalent of offering flights to the moon.

The first step in being Commercial is to articulate a strategy and strategic plan.

MOONSHOT MATURITY MODEL

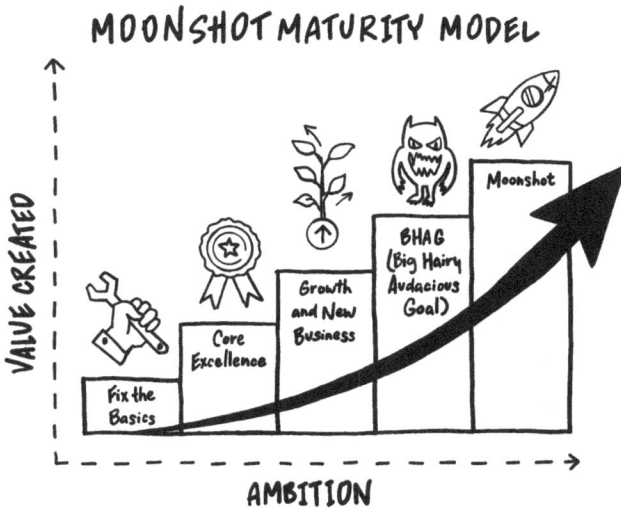

A strategy and strategic plan will help your organisation focus and deliver impact. It will allow a level of control and ownership of the direction and dramatically improve the opportunity to profit. The strategy will set out the longer-term vision of the organisation and set out to understand all the various dynamics that will influence the outcome. The strategic plan will identify the steps to get from here to there, and help you navigate your way through the environment. Both the strategy and strategic plan will help guide you when you need to make hard decisions, particularly in a disruptive environment.

WHAT YOU CAN DO

☑ Get very clear on why you are in business and what business you are in;

☑ Articulate your values and allow them to show you how to achieve your strategy;

☑ Establish a well-articulated strategy and strategic plan, with the right level of engagement, which become living documents embraced by the organisation;

☑ Set your priorities so that your expansion is manageable; and

☑ Utilise the Moonshot Maturity Model to place structure, and sequence, around your ambition.

CHAPTER 2

BUILD GOOD GOVERNANCE

A KEY ELEMENT OF STRONG COMMERCIAL PERFORMANCE IS TO HAVE strong governance and control systems in place. Intuitively, you may think that governance slows a business down and limits the creative process. But the right governance framework will help you maintain control as you grow. Strong commercial business performers have very strong governance because it gives them a structure and platform that allows them to be agile. The challenge, of course, is to get the balance right and to ensure that governance is placed at the right level – not too much and not too little.

SERVICE YOUR BRAKES

You should think of a business like a Formula 1 car. Formula 1 is one of the most innovative spaces known to humankind. Year on year, this sport is developing and innovating at a rapid rate. But to be successful, a Formula 1 car needs to have control. Without control, it would keep crashing. If the car kept crashing, all energies would be spent on *fixing* the car, not *improving* the car.

Everyone in an organisation needs to have a level of accountability and responsibility for good governance. If the organisation were to lose control, profit would be diminished, and service performance would suffer greatly – with everyone distracted by trying to understand what is wrong with the business.

One of the biggest risks is growing too fast without the governance, systems and controls in place to be able to cope. While it is possible to get away without these safeguards in the short term, the problems created by not having them will inevitably arise and place the organisation at significant risk.

Good governance comes from good systems of process and work. Having strong governance does not mean you have to be inefficient; in fact, it can help drive your efficiency by ensuring that you have all your systems in place to be able to cope with the pressure.

When creating and innovating for business, it is also imperative that the governance aspects of the business are considered in the design. This is not to slow the process down, but rather to give it the structure and foundation so that any growth can be achieved with sustainable success. Good governance will also maintain credibility in terms of an organisation's legal and ethical standing within the stakeholder community. Every organisation, no matter how big or small, has obligations far wider than itself. Illegal or unethical behaviour can be intentional, but can also occur unintentionally, due to accident, lack of awareness or a breakdown in process and communication. If an organisation breaches its legal or ethical credibility, it not only becomes distracting and affects performance, it is also wrong. All organisations must do business in the right way. Having a good governance framework will prevent unintended legal and ethical breaches.

The other critical aspect to strong governance is building transparency. Transparency is required to build confidence and trust, which, in turn, will support the ability to create, innovate and collaborate while maintaining commercial integrity. If the organisation or its stakeholders are questioning the information and truths expressed by the leadership, management will become crippled by having to explain and justify itself. Demonstrating good governance is a very strong indication that what is said is meant and will be done.

To illustrate how bad things can get without good governance, consider the fate of blood testing start-up Theranos, which was founded by Elizabeth Holmes. In 2015, the business had a valuation of USD$9 billion, yet, some three years later, Ms Holmes had stepped down as CEO after being charged with fraud, and the business folded in the same year. This was despite having former Secretaries of State Henry Kissinger and George Shultz on the board. What happened? Media and commentary allege the vision of Theranos and the stories that they were telling investors and media were not matching reality. The technology they were suggesting they had did not yet exist, although they were frantically trying to develop it. Staff at all levels were raising concerns, but they were either fired or silenced. The lies became so big that they became self-perpetuating. The organisation, the CEO and the COO were under immense pressure to deliver results and support the level of funding that they were receiving. They apparently had to maintain the mistruths, but eventually it unravelled. All that investment, all that employment, all the opportunity was gone. They grew too quickly, they were not held to account, and they believed in their own rhetoric.

As you start launching new innovations, it is important to know that they are being delivered in the way that is anticipated. Without these strong controls, great innovations can just languish without the right focus, or they may become a massive distraction with unacceptable financial impacts.

Governance controls do not have to be overbearing; they can be as simple as:

- Having appropriate financial budgets, reporting and process established;
- Establishing an investment council that can independently review investment decisions;
- Having clear accountabilities and delineations for roles – particularly for senior management roles;
- Providing training and development in the areas of ethics, responsible business management and leadership;
- Putting in place appropriate measures and safeguards to ensure the integrity of data and information;
- Establishing a risk management framework, and periodically reviewing the effectiveness of the framework;
- Remunerating sensibly and fairly; and
- Having an adequate and independent internal audit program in place.

BALANCE RISK WITH OPPORTUNITY

The world has a lot of moving parts and the commercial world can sometimes be brutal. There are many risks out there, particularly for new business and when executing improvement initiatives. You cannot risk what you cannot afford, but, equally, you can't sit inside behind closed doors in constant fear that you may be run over or catch a cold. To be commercial you must balance risk with opportunity. But how do you do that?

Risks can be mitigated if you spend time working through them sensibly. We can't possibly know every risk that will emerge, but what we can do is be prepared. Know how we will react and respond, know where we could call on resources, know how to protect ourselves. The key is having the play book already sorted out, and not just for a specific situation, but for any situation.

A Formula 1 car is built to deal with multiple environments. Racetracks are all different – some have many corners; some have more straights. F1 cars are designed to cope with different temperatures and weather conditions, such as dry or wet, hot or cold. Teams will not know the conditions until the day of the race – but they are prepared for it.

Risk management is a fundamental business discipline, but the same level of time and focus should be put into opportunity management. Don't leave value on the table because you're so focused on what can go wrong that that you don't prepare yourself for making the most of opportunities that arise.

You need to find the balance between talking yourself out of doing something and finding reasons why you *can* do it. Our default position as humans will always be to find reasons why we cannot do something, so we must be consciously aware of that and make an enormous effort to build a positive, can-do mind set. One way to do this is to have an opportunity plan.

Being prepared for any opportunity or eventuality gets back to the heart of being adaptable and ensuring that an organisation can act appropriately, and in its own best interests, during a difficult event. Part of the challenge is to keep going during these times. The resilience that is required to push through these barriers is important so that you can survive and prosper in the new age. Business is full of uncertainty, more so now than ever before, and companies that can manage that uncertainty will be the ones that succeed.

Opportunity capability is a core skill that an organisation must have so that it can not only respond to the changing environment and the opportunities that it presents, but also be able to shape the opportunity environment for themselves. It is as much of a risk not to respond to key opportunities that can deliver significant value as it is to chase the wrong ones – ones that become distracting and wasteful to the organisation.

Let's quickly review some of the key elements of risk management, with one eye on opportunities:

- Train and develop your staff so that they have the skill not only to respond to risk, but to proactively manage it and turn it into a competitive advantage. Train them to be able to differentiate between opportunity and risk;
- Understand the various scenarios that may play out, along with the financial, people and customer consequences. Rank those in terms of risk, likelihood and level of impact;
- Have contingency plans in place and practise them;
- Seek independent advice. Sometimes it just takes a person who is not involved in the day to day of operations to be able to see the blatant risks and opportunities;
- Give your team time to proactively manage risks and

opportunities. If they are constantly under-resourced, it is unlikely that they will be able to identify or manage risks effectively; and

- Be comfortable that the world is an uncertain place, and help your team have resilience and the understanding that it is sometimes necessary to change course.

STATE YOUR (BUSINESS) CASE

In a disruptive environment, opportunities may pop up at any time, but how do you decide which opportunities to pursue? That's where it's important to have the capacity to conduct a business case assessment quickly, thoroughly and accurately.

When opportunities are presented, it is wise to work through an appropriate business case process. This is particularly true when opportunities either require the investment of significant resources or can provide significant value to the organisation. The business case will demonstrate that the opportunity has been well thought through and that it is aligned with the business strategy.

The business case is also another opportunity to become very clear on the vision of the initiative, and how it will provide value to the customer and to the organisation. If an idea of value is not worth the time and effort required to develop a sound business case, there is probably a lack of commitment to the opportunity. This in itself may indicate that investing in it would be a wasteful and futile exercise.

The business case process does not have to be slow, particularly if the organisation has a standard approach that is resourced appropriately. In fact, it can help inform the idea and solution generation.

The business case should consider many of the following key elements:

1. The vision and purpose of the initiative
2. The impact to the customer, stakeholders and organisation
3. The intended execution and delivery paths
4. The timelines of the initiative
5. The resources required to bring the innovation to light
6. Risks and opportunities assessment
7. Key financial information and timings, including, but not limited to:
   a. Key assumptions, such as interest and inflation rates
   b. A baseline, as a starting point
   c. Expected incremental revenues
   d. Expected incremental costs
   e. Project costs – both capital and operational
   f. Cashflow impacts
   g. Net present value calculation (or another capital investment calculation that will demonstrate wise allocation of capital, and consideration of the time value of money)
   h. Sensitivity analysis

The business case process should not take away from the creative process; it must be designed to aid it. If the process becomes bureaucratised, not only will it slow innovation, it will also deflate the spirit and trust of the teams that are generating the ideas and solutions. What the business case does have to do is ensure that any investment and allocation of resource is aligned with the strategic intent, capacity and capability of the organisation so that there is an effective use of resources and focus.

A business case for innovation requires significant communication effort to be able to help decision makers understand the long-term imperatives of resetting culture and investing in certain innovations that will protect and help you thrive in periods of disruption. If you cannot make the case, the whole organisation may be steered down a path that will jeopardise its future. The business case will help tell the story of how innovation will support the long-term strategy of the organisation.

MANAGE YOUR MONEY

So, now that we have good governance in place to protect our business, a way of balancing risk with opportunity, and a well-practised ability to quickly and accurately make a business case assessment, we need to ensure that cash is available so we can leap on a sound opportunity as soon as it pops up.

To be commercial, you must ensure that your capital allocation towards innovative initiatives doesn't bring your normal operations to a gridlock because there are insufficient funds to operate. However, it's also senseless if you can't make cash available to a committed initiative. Once again, it's about balance.

If you do not manage your cashflow properly, you simply will not have a business, nor will you be able to invest in innovation. There have been many good businesses, even profitable ones, which have not survived because they have been unable to manage cashflow.

You will need to understand the big picture – when cash movements will take place, and when you will need to call upon your cash reserves or finance the liquidity of your business.

Cash keeps the wheels turning, both for existing operations and for new initiatives. Both can be placed at significant risk if strong cashflow disciplines are not followed.

It also pays to remember that unless you get paid by your customer in a timely fashion, they are not an actual customer – they are a resource drain. Equally, if you are not paying your suppliers in a reasonable timeframe, then it would be difficult for you to develop deep and meaningful relationships with them that can add value through the innovation process.

Wise investment is also essential for good governance that makes your business commercial. As you change, reset, transform or innovate your business, you will probably need to make certain upfront investments.

You may need new plant and equipment or new software, or you may need to invest in the development of a new product and its associated manpower costs. You may need to do some restructuring in order to set your business up for growth – this may include redundancies, exiting lease premises or ceasing to use certain processes, equipment or software.

The objective is to identify the option that can deliver the highest return for the capital invested. The organisation needs to consider its investment decisions against numerous conditions, such as an expected rate of return, the time value of money (net present value) and the risk profile of an investment.

Cash flows and the business environment can be difficult to predict, particularly in the long term. Flawed assumptions can mean that initial outlay will not be recovered. Even with the most carefully determined assumptions, and the most astute capital investment modelling, we can never really predict the future. Anyone can be caught out by a freak event such as the global financial crisis, and we are seeing industries being annihilated now through digital disruption and the onset of global trade wars. So it makes sense to complete sensitivity analyses on your models to determine both the positive and negative impacts of incorrect assumptions.

Organisations need to decide between competing investment decisions, and must prioritise how they use their cash resource. The base position will always be putting the money in the bank or returning funds to shareholders. Investment decisions need to be considered against the options that are available and the risk appetite of the organisation.

Every dollar invested – each site, each geography, each piece of equipment, each product, each inventory item – needs to pull its weight and deliver a return.

A strong and healthy balance sheet is essential if you are going to be able to manage disruption, and it should have the following characteristics:

- Intelligent and productive working capital;
- Positive cash flow;
- A balanced and right-sized capital structure; and
- Income-generating assets.

If you do not have a strong balance sheet, you will find it hard to defend against disruption activity as you will not be able to withstand the initial profit and cash impact, and, most importantly, you will not have the capacity to invest in innovation initiatives that will help you thrive in a period of disruption. Also, by focusing on your balance sheet, you will ensure you do not erode value in your profit improvement initiatives.

The second step to being Commercial is to build a governance framework.

A governance framework will help your organisation keep control during periods of growth and uncertainty. It will also be important to ensure that the right level of diligence and structure is placed around key investment decisions and that the organisation does not become cash depleted as it grows. Importantly, the governance framework will be as much about opportunity as it is about risk, and will have the structure to accelerate great opportunities

WHAT YOU CAN DO TO BUILD GOOD GOVERNANCE

- ☑ Review current gaps in your governance framework;
- ☑ Develop risk and opportunity plans with mitigations or intensification, accountabilities and impact levels;
- ☑ Establish a structured way of assessing opportunity through a business case framework;
- ☑ Manage cashflows effectively; and
- ☑ Establish strong financial controls and review frameworks, cadence and reviews.

CHAPTER 3

DESIGN AN EFFECTIVE BUSINESS INTELLIGENCE CAPABILITY

IF YOU WANT TO BE A PROFITABLE PLAYER IN A DISRUPTIVE BUSI-ness environment, you need information – lots of it. But you also need accurate information, and you need to receive that information quickly – in real time if possible. This is an area that is changing rapidly, and you need to have your finger on the pulse of changing technologies that deliver information and be able to utilise them.

Most importantly, you need to use the right information, and have it delivered the right way. You will not be a commercial business if your business reporting gets you bogged down in irrelevant information and verbose, inefficient reports. Being commercial is about being agile and efficient, and business information should support that, not prevent it. Your organisation needs a source of objective business intelligence that will help its leaders make more timely and accurate decisions. To do this there needs to be a method for combining data-driven realities with intuitive and creative assumptions, perspectives and solutions.

STAY ON TRACK

To be effective, leaders and operators must know their numbers. This is at the heart of being a commercial business. The most basic, tried and tested way to do this is to use key performance indicators (KPIs). KPIs are not sexy, and they're nothing new, but you must use them in a way that allows you to be an agile, forward-looking and innovative business.

Key performance indicators provide a measurable insight into how effective an organisation is in achieving its key strategic goals and operational imperatives. While you will need KPIs at various levels, and within functions and operations, the first rule must be that they all connect to the strategic goal of the organisation. If they do not connect and the wrong thing is measured, they won't assist you in achieving your strategic goals, even if you have a positive KPI outcome.

The value of KPIs as a communication tool cannot be underestimated. Your KPIs should be easy to discuss and communicate at all levels of the organisation, and you want outsiders to be able to look at your KPIs and easily understand the primary performance.

The word 'key' is no accident. A KPI is not trying to measure everything; it is trying to measure what matters most. The objective is to find those indicators that, when met, mean the business is doing well. Or, conversely, when those same indicators are not being met, you know that the organisation may be at risk. Selecting the wrong KPIs can have you monitoring the wrong things.

Of course, the number of KPIs you need will depend on the size and complexity of your organisation. Any more than five or six for each key function, activity or person may be counterproductive. You don't want to feel like you're sitting in the cockpit of an aircraft with dozens of instruments that need checking and monitoring; you want your KPI reports to have the simplicity and feel of sitting in the driver's seat of your car.

From a change perspective, many employees become nervous if you develop ridiculous or misaligned KPIs that they must deliver despite having limited control or influence over their outcomes. Worse is when you set the KPI without employee engagement. You may find that you're on separate paths with limited alignment, and the actions do not complement the intent. Sometimes this is simply due to misunderstanding.

KPIs bring accountability, visibility and transparency. This can sometimes make employees nervous, but if they're set correctly, they will be strongly welcomed and embraced. People thrive on accountability, and they like to know when they are doing a great job. They also like to know when others are letting the team down and are not making fair contributions. While KPIs are not tools for naming, blaming and shaming, there will be an element of transparency and visibility that will ensure that teams and individuals who are not engaged or are performing poorly can't hide behind a curtain of confusion.

Your KPIs don't need to be fixed. As you achieve them and have them well within control, or as your strategic intentions change, it is important to ensure that your KPIs grow and change as well.

BE DIGITAL

There is no excuse for not being digital in today's rapidly changing business environment. Digital technologies are a key reason why that environment is being disrupted, and you must harness that technology and make it work for you. Being digital means that you can execute faster, access better and more timely information, and create new and more meaningful ways to engage your customers, team members and stakeholders.

Good digital applications will speed the business up, provide richer data sources, make it easy for all stakeholders to interact with your business, and push inefficiencies and waste out of your business. Freed-up resources generated through digital transformation can then be deployed on working on activities that add value. This is a better use of resource, which can be allocated to initiatives that will support the long-term sustainability of the organisation.

Customers will insist on working with your organisation digitally and, as the new work force takes shape, one of the prerequisites for attracting talent will be to ensure that you are operating in a modern setting. People simply will not want to work for you if you are not digitally enabled and it will become increasingly difficult to work with your suppliers. Information exchanges along the supply chain are key to building consistency, efficiency and stability for any organisation.

There are many different levels that you can go to when it comes to systems and digital capability, but it is important that you focus on getting the basics right first. Focus on what matters most and then build from there.

Many digital applications also have lots of glitter and little substance, so critical evaluation needs to be made about why you need a system, what you hope to get from it and how you are going to implement or operate it.

Transitioning to become a leading player in the digital space is nothing short of enormous, however, as overwhelming as it may appear, the path is a lot simpler when you have the organisation aligned with becoming digitally ready and everybody understands the reasons why this is so important. There is probably no better motivator than survival, and organisations that do not go digital will not survive.

EMBRACE EMERGING TECHNOLOGIES

It is essential to be digital in business today. But you also need to be positioned to take advantage of the digital capabilities of tomorrow. Data analytics can now be done with greater speed and efficiency than before. Computer processing capability has risen exponentially, as have abilities to connect and make sense of varying and disconnected data sources, in particular, social media data sources. If analytics are applied properly to big data and unstructured data sources, immense value can be unlocked.

In the past, organisations have gathered information, run analytics, uncovered some insights based on historical data and then applied that to future situations. Today, that process can be completed much faster and with greater accuracy, and often can be managed in real time. Being able to make these analyses quickly means that the information used to inform decisions is newer, fresher and more relevant. This promotes commercial agility because companies can align themselves with their customers' needs almost as soon as those needs have changed, rather than forever playing catch-up. But it goes even further.

The objective now is to move to predicting rather than explaining. Data science is a blend of various tools, algorithms and machine-learning principles aimed at discovering hidden patterns from the raw data. While data analytics simply provides an explanation of a situation based on the processing of historical data, data science uses advanced methods to predict that an event will occur in the future. The data will be considered from many angles, not just a historical one, and be able to establish patterns and relationships that could not previously be discovered.

The internet of things, big data, blockchain, artificial intelligence and machine learning are still in their infancy, but the pace at which these things are being tested, adopted and developed is significant. There will be many organisations playing in this space with not a lot of idea why they are doing it or what they are hoping to achieve, let alone how to do it properly and effectively. But those organisations that do understand and can apply new technology to solve customer problems or enhance the customer experience will gain significant advantage.

Organisations need to move fast to build this capability, not just because it is necessary to meet modern demands, but also to shore up resources. There will be a shortage of skilled resources as the digital revolution shifts to an exponential growth rate.

Key steps that you should consider taking are:

1. Develop a deep understanding of modern technologies that will assist your organisation;
2. Understand your customers' and your organisation's digital needs;
3. Partner with organisations that have digital knowledge and capability – this can help accelerate your capability gap;
4. Eliminate concepts that are not relevant to your organisation, so that you are not distracted trying to implement something that is either of no benefit or which your organisation is not ready for;
5. Prioritise the key digital capabilities that you require;
6. Develop a plan;
7. Test and learn; and
8. Make it happen.

BEWARE OF ANALYSIS PARALYSIS

It's important to have good quality business intelligence supporting your business, and part of this is not getting bogged down in decision making through over-analysing data and over-thinking decisions. A commercial business makes swift, efficient, well-supported decisions. The biggest risk to strong commercial governance and performance is paralysis by analysis. Many organisations get themselves into a situation where they are producing too much data, generating too many reports, and measuring everything other than what really counts.

Today, when we are data and information rich, the risk of being paralysed by too much information is even greater. There are many systems that can do wonderful things, such as give real-time insights, but massive effort is sometimes required to set these up and they often don't produce the outcome that was expected or desired.

Running a successful and commercially performing business means *not* getting buried in generating reports. It's *not* looking for information, reviewing the wrong information, sorting through too much information or getting caught in a vicious cycle of explaining variances and performance rather than doing what is required to fix faulty performance.

Good businesses have very solid management information systems in place where the right information is being filtered to the right people, in the right volume, at the right time and in the right place. Anything else becomes paralysing. People will fix problems, so the management information system needs to support good decision making and problem solving, not hinder it.

WHAT DOES GOOD BUSINESS INTELLIGENCE LOOK LIKE?

Management reporting and analysis will only be as good as the work and investment that goes into creating it. Often these reports and dashboards take too long to produce, fail to tell the whole story, fail to engage the users and audience in the process, or have skewed results based on the bias of the person producing the report. All of this makes them meaningless. They can be both irrelevant and complex, yet, developing them can consume a huge amount of company resources. Preparing them can become distracting and time-consuming for all involved or, worse, the reports can make representations that lead to flawed decision making.

So, what are the characteristics of good business intelligence?

It looks good

It is critical that the information is presented in a visually pleasing format so that the user can quickly understand the message. The human mind cannot process too much data at once without getting overwhelmed. Getting overwhelmed leads to decision fatigue, which makes it harder for your management team to think strategically. Clarity should be the primary objective of your reports and dashboards. You don't want people debating the intent or, worse, the integrity of the report or dashboard. Follow good design principles so your reports capture the reader's attention and can be easily understood.

It's simple

I once worked in a business that was absolutely crippled by the level of reporting they were doing. The reports were so complicated that you needed to be a Rhodes Scholar to understand them, and they were neither intuitive nor presented in a way that supported quick and informed decision making. Unsurprisingly, about ninety-nine per cent of them were never looked at. The team would have been producing in excess of 100 reports, but only one or two were key. The time and effort it took to produce the reports could have been better utilised elsewhere.

It's relevant

Management reporting systems need to measure strategic and operational performance and set benchmarks for what great performance looks like. They must help the organisation to learn and act quickly on the insight. The best information is available in real time and can influence positive action. This may be only a small pivot from course, or it could highlight a massive iceberg in the distance that must be avoided. For it to be relevant, it needs to be timely – preferably real time.

It's transparent

You want the information to be transparent and accessible to everyone in the organisation. While some information, such as payroll data, will be sensitive, you want as many people as possible to understand and engage with the management information. Having one version of the truth enables everyone to be on the same page and, therefore, limits meaningless debate.

It's unbiased

It's important that the analysis is not subject to bias and is able to tell a complete picture.

I once worked for an organisation going through a massive transformation, and some of the analysis presented to the executives had two problems. The first was that it only analysed the impact on one function, not the business as a whole. When analysing the end-to-end impact on the organisation, the analysis told a very different story.

The second problem was that it was authored by a person who would benefit from agreement to the proposition expressed. The analysis was not objective at all, and while it was not malicious or deliberately dishonest, it was tainted, and the executive team were none the wiser. It was only picked up before it was too late because a new team member was strong enough to raise the flag.

Therefore, whole-of-business, holistic performance measures need to be adopted.

It tells a story

The information has to tell a story. It needs to capture the reader's attention and help them understand what is happening and what action is required. Without this meaning and connection, the information will simply be a bunch of numbers and graphs.

Operators and leaders need to be able to 'talk to the numbers' in a simple and concise manner. This can only be made possible if the information that they are relying on to communicate is simple and concise itself. The information needs to add support or weight to the narrative, not distract from the key message being delivered.

> The third step in being Commercial is to design a business intelligence capability

Business intelligence will provide the organisation's leaders, management and operations with key insights so that they know when they are on track, whether they need to pivot, or whether they are about to hit an iceberg. It will also tell them if they're about to miss a massive opportunity. The information should support proactive decision making so that action is taken in time to leverage the situation.

WHAT YOU CAN DO

☑ Establish a KPI and management reporting framework that is simple, intuitive and focuses on (or brings attention to) the things that matter most;

☑ Have a digital transition plan in place with consideration of what will create efficiency and impact for your customers and your organisation;

☑ Build relationships with technology providers who will be able to add value, and review best-practice solutions across your industry and other industries; and

☑ Carefully consider what information you will stop generating so that you can bring focus to the important information and help everybody to cut through the noise and be on the same page.

CHAPTER 4

MAKE EVERY DOLLAR COUNT

THE TITLE OF THIS BOOK IS 'FIT FOR DISRUPTION'. IT'S ABOUT HOW to improve your profits in a disruptive, rapidly changing world. But there are no magic bullets. It would be nice to be the next Facebook or make a billion dollars overnight, but even Mark Zuckerberg has to do the accounts. The first attribute of the Fit for Disruption model – be Commercial – is all about getting the basics right. You might think you know everything there is to know about a profit improvement program, that you've heard all this before, but just humour me while we go over the basics again. You might be surprised just how well these foundational practices will set you up to seize the 'next big thing' when it appears on the horizon.

ELIMINATE WASTE

Have you ever had to change the tyre on your car, or watch someone do it? There are many steps involved and, depending on how well set up you were, the task would probably have taken fifteen minutes. Now put your mind to changing the tyre of a Formula 1 car. In Formula 1, it takes less than two seconds to change four tyres. The necessary tools must be available and in good working order, and even the driver contributes by making sure he stops in exactly the right spot. This process has effectively been a waste-elimination exercise. All non-value-adding activity has been removed and all the value-add activity has surfaced. Process changes and appropriate technology have also been introduced to make this astonishing feat possible. And the teams are still trying to reduce the time – while this seems impossible, that fraction of a second may be the difference between winning and losing in a multibillion-dollar industry.

Waste is any activity that absorbs resources but does not add value. An activity does not add value if your customer is not willing to pay for it or to pay more for it. Value must always be determined from the customer's point of view. Waste costs your business and your customer money, time and resources. Resources can include people, time, equipment, material and space – it can also include opportunity, because a focus on one initiative may be at the expense of another.

It is not hard to identify and eliminate waste; we do it all day every day. We find the shortest way to get to work, the best time to catch up with someone, the best-value air ticket, or the best retail product to purchase. My children are great at both generating waste and eliminating it. Whenever they have a chore that must be done, they will find the quickest, easiest way to do it. Bill Gates has said, '*I will always choose a lazy person to do a difficult job because a lazy person will find an easy way to do it.*'

Your organisation needs to be trained on how to identify and eliminate waste. First, it needs to be understood which activities create value, which tasks are non-value-adding but necessary, and which are simply non-value-adding. Non-value-adding tasks should be eliminated immediately, and you should endeavour to innovate your processes so that necessary non-value-add activities can be turned into non-value-add activities, which can then be eliminated.

There are typically eight forms of process waste – waste that is generated by inefficient processes. There are also six forms of resource waste – waste generated by having underutilised or ineffective people on staff.

Process waste
- Overproduction: Producing sooner or in greater quantities than the customers demand
- Waiting: Underutilising people or items while a process completes a work cycle
- Transportation: Moving items or people between processes unnecessarily
- Over-processing: Unnecessary processes that do not contribute to value flow
- Inventory: Generating material that does not add value
- Rework: Repeating or correcting a process
- Motion: Essential moving of items or people between processes
- Intellect: Failure to fully utilise the time and talents of people

Resource waste
- Unavailable: Resources are often not available when the work needs to be done
- Task switching: Switching tasks inefficiently can cause excessive time waste
- Working slow: People not having the best method, motivation or training

- Interruptions: Work interrupted by issues that don't add value
- Start-up: Time wasted at the start of the day or shift
- Causing defects/errors: Doing work that has to be corrected or reworked

If you want to be a commercial business, you should review your operations with the above list in mind.

ELIMINATE WASTE

PROCESS WASTE

1. Overproduction
2. Waiting
3. Transportation
4. Overprocessing
5. Inventory
6. Rework
7. Motion
8. Intellect

RESOURCE WASTE

1. Unavailable
2. Task switching
3. Working slow
4. Interruptions
5. Start-up
6. Causing defects/errors

CHECK THE INVOICES

As I said, even Mark Zuckerberg has to do the accounts. Well, someone, in fact, a team, probably does them for him. And he and his team most certainly check their invoices.

The obvious benefit of checking invoices is to ensure that the activity has been completed and you have been charged the right rate. We all know that suppliers can become a little cheeky with their invoicing, and if they go unchecked it just gives a supplier licence to keep conducting themselves in this way – whether intentional or not.

But invoices are also very useful to identify where you are doing operationally stupid things. I once did a review of invoices and noticed that we were sending one pallet of inventory to a retail store hundreds of kilometres away but paying for a full truck load when there was capacity for at least another twenty-three pallets. I was unsure whether the carrier was double dipping by loading up with cargo from other customers and charging them as well, or whether they were just sending a half-empty truck. Regardless, why our organisation would be sending one pallet at a time was confusing, as it only had to be consolidated with other stock or the timing of the flow altered.

The service provider has a role to play here, and it is unconscionable for them to allow you to do operationally stupid things. It is near on criminal if they are exploiting that situation to capitalise commercially for themselves. The problem may not be the service provider's fault, but there should be an onus on them not to allow it to happen.

Reviewing the invoices can also help you see whether you're using services that are adding no value to the customer. This can happen as a legacy when operations have been left unmonitored.

Checking invoices should never be a substitute for walking the operations and seeing for yourself exactly what's happening at the coalface, but it will help to complete the picture of your reviews.

CUT THE RIGHT COSTS

Reviewing costs and finding places where you can trim the fat is obviously a core part of any profit improvement program. Excess slows you down; being trim helps you respond to opportunities and threats in a disruptive environment. But be careful – if cutting costs, you have to make sure you cut the right ones.

Focus on the costs that matter most. Do not focus on the stationery spend when your cost of goods sold or your cost of sales is causing you to haemorrhage. Do not focus on your uniform costs when, in fact, you have a wages and salary cost blow-out. Do not focus on cutting your toilet paper or heating budget when your logistics costs are out of control and you are shipping product to the wrong place in the wrong quantity at the wrong time. Focus on what will make the most difference.

Focus on the variable costs first – not the small fish but the big fish. Focus on what costs you can control, and which will have an impact on your bottom line. Look at what costs make up the greatest percentage. Product costs, wages and salaries, logistics and supply chain are generally great places to start.

You need to understand what is driving the cost: is it volume, rate or both? However, that is not the total picture; questions need to be asked about why you are incurring the cost in the first place. Can things be done differently? Are you able to streamline your process or can you even eliminate the need to incur the cost without affecting service? Maybe you are incurring high overtime costs because you have not balanced your operation; maybe you have high transport costs because you are over-servicing a customer; perhaps you are spending more on raw materials because your procurement team have too close a relationship with your supplier; or maybe you don't have an adequate rostering system to manage peak periods.

When you are looking at entering into large fixed-cost arrangements, such as property, be extra diligent. Do some extra analysis, get better market research and seek external advice to make sure that you get this one right. When you are locked into a very large contract for a very long time, it becomes very difficult to manage on a period-by-period basis.

Understand what you can control and when you can control it. For instance, look at your power and energy costs and absolutely make sure you negotiate a great rate, but don't sit there analysing it every month when it will not change, and the cost is the cost.

Also, make sure you don't cut costs where doing so will cut value. For example, a mistake many organisations make is trying to scrimp and save when it comes to getting good people. If you want monkeys, pay peanuts. It will be much better having one great person in your organisation than ten average people. Focus on the quality, and on the return. There is no point employing someone who gives a negative return, yet, many organisations take this course because it's cheaper.

Spend what you have to spend to add value, and don't spend on anything that adds no value. Be careful, because how you spend sends all sorts of signals to the market. For example, if you are not controlled, suppliers will soon be aware of this and try to charge higher prices because the culture allows it. Equally, if you are cutting costs where it is important, this will only annoy customers, which will ultimately erode value.

CONSIDER END-TO-END COSTS

It is important that you consider costs in totality. While it's not practical, ideally, you would look at every product and every service and understand what it truly costs to produce. This should include costs such as logistics, management, offices, systems, accounting fees and the like. If each individual product or service were a business on its own, would it make or lose money for you?

I have been in a retail setting where products worth less than $5.00 would be picked, packed and despatched at unit level from the distribution centre. The cost to complete that activity would erode more than just the margin, and in many instances the costs outstripped the sell price of the product. Sometimes the company packed a single pair of socks in a carton full of air and sent them from China to a remote store that already had plenty of these socks in stock.

It's important to consider context, of course. Airfreight is an expensive option, but for a high-end fashion brand, where it is necessary to have speed to market, airfreight could absolutely be appropriate. For a low-cost discount retailer, however, it would be very unlikely that airfreight could ever be justified.

To understand end-to-end costs, you need to understand your complete supply chain. The old adage of getting it right first time rings true. If you get your supply chain optimised at the start of the chain, it will save costs down the chain. If you don't control at source, your cost impact will just snowball and costs will exponentially increase at every touch point.

DON'T BE PENNY WISE AND POUND FOOLISH

Not all costs should be cut. Don't fall into the trap of becoming such a scrooge that you endanger both morale and the quality of your product or service.

Early in my career, when I was working with a large company, the CEO sent out a note that focused on cost control and which deflated the mood of the entire organisation and completely destroyed employee engagement. His note talked about watching every penny and making sure we spent wisely, including cancelling all travel. He then insisted that we squeeze more from our suppliers or service providers. But the part that just lost everyone was when he said we should consider the amount of toilet paper we were using. Now, I'm sure he was exaggerating to make a point, but the damage he made with this comment was irreparable. Whatever money was saved on travel or toilet paper was certainly nothing compared with the lost engagement, motivation and productivity caused by making such statements. It was foolish, regardless of the intention.

Not all costs should be squeezed – you need to spend money on travel if you are a business with geographically fragmented operations, for example. And remember that you can go too far – squeezing suppliers to the nth degree will just alienate them. Some organisations focus on driving the unit price down, only to get an uncooperative supplier and poor-quality product. I know of a grocery retailer that saved millions on the plastic bags provided in the fruit and vegetable department. But these bags were not sealed at the bottom, and if you placed a carrot in the bag it would fall straight though. Quality was compromised for price, and, ultimately, the cost of this decision far outweighed the original saving. Another example is squeezing service providers so hard that you have service failures. Some organisations will stop training teams or stop reinvesting in updating equipment or environments to keep them current. That is not a strategy for innovation, longevity or competitive advantage.

Trying to save money can become ridiculously counterproductive. For example, someone might refuse to invest $10,000 in capital that would generate $100,000 in benefit. In other words, they'd be willing to leave $100,000 on the table to save $10,000, ultimately incurring a $90,000 opportunity cost. Believe it or not, this happens.

It is also critically important to be allocating enough financial resource for capital funding. Transport companies need to update and maintain a current fleet, retail stores need to have fresh environments, manufacturers require plant and equipment to be updated. Funds need to be available to take advantage of current technology and digital upgrades. Sometimes an organisation needs to acquire another business or spend money on R&D. Organisations have to invest in the future, and while there may not be an immediate or obvious return, without capital investment your organisation will struggle to stay relevant.

You do have to spend money to make money. Just spend it wisely.

NEGOTIATE EVERYTHING

Don't forget that everything is negotiable, all the time. A lot of people will think that once a contract is signed, then that is it. A contract is a static document, a reflection of an agreement at a point in time, and something that you will probably never look at again after you've signed it.

Circumstances do change, however, and they change for all the contracted parties. The economic climate differs, the market conditions change, strategies change, people change, prosperity even changes. After time, assumptions in the contract may no longer be valid, or the interpretation may differ based on new circumstances. It is very impractical for a contract to include a contingency for every situation and every circumstance, but it should have mechanisms in place to deal with changing circumstances.

Don't find yourself in a ridiculous situation where both you and the other party in a contract would benefit from doing something different. Have the conversation.

It may be that a new process has been found which dramatically improves efficiency, but the contract was written in a way that the service provider gets all the upside. It would not hurt having the conversation to renegotiate a more balanced outcome, particularly if both parties are wanting to develop a long-term partnership. If the other party doesn't come to the table, then it would be fair to say they are focused on the short term and likely to move on. The focus here is for both parties to act in good faith and support each other to be successful.

It is not always appropriate to renegotiate a contract. You should not try to renegotiate simply because you have destroyed another area of your business and you need to find cost savings somewhere else. Do not exert undue pressure or power. That is a very short-term approach and can destroy trust, not only with the supplier or service provider in question but also others. However, where it works for both parties, work together to get the right solution. Don't be limited by a contract constraint – get creative.

Remember also that in any negotiation the aim is to increase the size of the pie, not slice it. Too often people get caught up in ensuring that they have the largest slice of the pie or that they protect what they have, rather than looking for creative ways of adding more value. It is nonsensical to want one hundred per cent of a pie that is smaller than, say, fifty per cent of a large pie. People lose focus on value, and attention is mistakenly turned to winning at the expense of the other party. The intention should always be to win/win. Of course, there will be times when you come up against someone who wants to negotiate on a win/lose basis, but the lesson here is simple; they should not be your partner and are not worth negotiating with if that is their attitude.

RESPECT YOUR SUPPLIERS' AND SERVICE PROVIDERS' PROFITS

It's important to respect your suppliers and service providers. You must work with them to get the best outcome for your business, and you can go down the very strong procurement route and just beat them into submission on price, but, ultimately, price will not be where the game is won. Nor do you want to pay more than fair value for something. Pay for value.

Understand and attack the suppliers' cost base. You must look at their business as if it were your own, or, better, as if both businesses were one, and understand where the value is. It is likely that the way you are doing business is actually imposing unnecessary cost on them;

maybe they are adding something to the good or service that is not required, or maybe you can help them find better sources, or more appropriate sources. It could be that they have a production line issue, or a management information issue; they may even be trying to transport or deliver the service in the wrong region.

Your suppliers and service providers are in business as much as you are, and they also have a right to make a profit. It would be naïve to think that you could prosper without your suppliers being prosperous also. If you attack your suppliers' costs and do not help support their profit (along with your profit), how do you expect them to partner in innovation?

RESTRUCTURE

So far in this chapter we've been talking about costs. But cost is about more than price. The structure of your organisation can also have a bearing on efficiency. In this case, less is more. When you add layers of management or throw people at problems, the operation becomes inefficient and slow. It also becomes overly complex for the people within the organisation, its partners and, importantly, its customers. But if you're going to restructure, you have to approach the process with great care.

A restructure can be a very stressful time for everyone involved and can expose your business to a great deal of risk, including loss of valuable knowledge, loss of engagement and loss of productivity. A restructure requires careful planning and must be linked to the strategic objectives of the organisation.

Restructures can also be met with a great deal of scepticism, as they often appear to be tokenistic and action for the sake of action. Shuffling the deckchairs has no real influence on improving performance.

That said, over time, organisations can accumulate excess in their organisational structure that does not serve them. Perhaps the excess was initially introduced to resolve an immediate need that no longer exists, or to cater for a now redundant process, or maybe it was set up to try to meet a strategic objective that is no longer relevant.

More management layers mean more decision points, and more required alignment. It does not add to the company's agility, nor does it simplify decision making. It is likely to mean more processes, more meetings, more potential for error in judgement.

As technology is introduced, labour requirements will change, and it does not help anyone to have people in roles that do not add value to the organisation or themselves. It will only add to a deepened anxiety as the culture becomes more about protecting a role than adding value.

While it is unfortunate that some businesses will need to downsize because they have lost market share and relevance, the Fit for Disruption method is about creating value and growth. If you control your commercials well, create new products, services and markets, and implement the change successfully, you will have growth. This will all go towards creating further employment opportunities – it just won't be the same roles.

Whatever happens – whether people are made redundant or are relocated into other roles – the most important thing is respect. They are not numbers; they are people, and if you do not treat people well, you will compromise your engagement, your brand and your values.

The fourth step in being Commercial is to make every dollar count.

Having a profit improvement program will help focus the organisation on making every dollar count and eliminating waste. The profit improvement program will help the organisation focus on value, as opposed to revenue or costs in isolation, with a direct focus on the impact on the bottom line. The program will enable quick wins and establish long-term, sustainable solutions to ensure your organisation is geared to financially make the most of its opportunities.

WHAT YOU CAN DO

- ☑ Start a simplified, 'lean' initiative and education program to help everybody in your organisation be able to identify and eliminate waste;
- ☑ Review every line of your profit and loss to identify opportunity and areas of potential waste;
- ☑ Map your current supply chain (product or service) to identify where value is created; and
- ☑ Review every supplier, and their arrangements, with the view to consolidating the supplier base and renegotiating arrangements.

THE PRIZES OF BEING COMMERCIAL

The following embody the benefits of getting this attribute right:

Profitability

Profit is good. Profit is what is needed to be able to ensure sustainability and relevance. Profit can be reinvested into further opportunities. It is a very strong indication that you have relevance and efficiency built into your business. Profitability gives you access to better resources and the space and freedom to work on growth.

Purpose

Profit allows you to create opportunities for your people and the communities in which you operate. Providing opportunities for your people will lift their individual value, and also deepen their level of engagement with the business. It helps them develop and prosper, which is just reward for their contribution to organisational success. Contributing to the community creates a sense of purpose beyond pure commercial value.

Growth

Profit will generate cashflow that can be reinvested in the organisation. The organisation can lift the bar in terms of its purpose, and the reinvestment can be allocated to help support the achievement of that purpose. It will allow you to accelerate new ideas and to try new markets.

Efficiency

Profit and efficiency go hand in hand. If you are eliminating waste and running a lean operation that is primed to deliver great service at optimal cost, you are building additional value. This efficiency leads to faster outcomes and less confusion. You can get more done with less, and it is done in a way that is level and controlled.

Operational stability and excellence

When you are Commercial you have greater control, transparency and resources available to you. This, in turn, gives you greater capacity to stabilise your operations, and then establish excellence. This is important because unless you have stable operations, you will not be Fit for Disruption, as your energy and focus will be on stabilising, not innovating.

PART 2

CREATE NEW SOLUTIONS

THE SECOND ATTRIBUTE OF THE FIT FOR DISRUPTION MODEL IS CREATE. This is your ability to innovate and design commercial solutions that solve problems.

Profitable industry leaders are creative, and they are innovative. They are prepared to look at problems in new ways, to embrace different ideas, and to join dots that have previously remained disconnected. They create; they bring ideas to life. Infinite possibilities appear when we learn to collaborate and work with each other to develop solutions.

But we have to discipline our creativity. To create is to deliver value. If an effort does not create value, it is a pointless exercise. Removing limiting beliefs, opening the mind, and possibly the heart, will create value. Being creative does not mean you have to become the next Uber, Facebook or Google. It is simply about creating value for your organisation, your customers and your people. It may not be a product or service; you may create a new process that supports the back end of the business. To create, we just need a problem. It does not matter what the problem is, as long as we can choose the right problem and are able to define it.

The key steps to being able to **CREATE** new solutions that solve problems are:

1. Foster an environment that will boost **imagination** and provide opportunities for **creativity**;
2. Develop a **mindset** that supports your creativity;
3. Understand that you are in the business of **solving problems**, and that you should solve problems for your customer, not yourself; and
4. Start **learning by doing** – prepare to learn from many (small) failures and wins to move quickly.

1. FOSTER an ENVIRONMENT that will BOOST IMAGINATION and PROVIDE OPPORTUNITIES for CREATIVITY.

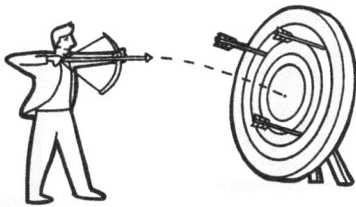

START LEARNING BY DOING — prepare to learn from many (small) failures and wins to move quickly.

4. CREATE MODEL

2. DEVELOP a MINDSET that SUPPORTS YOUR CREATIVITY.

3.

UNDERSTAND THAT YOU ARE IN THE BUSINESS OF SOLVING PROBLEMS, and that you should solve problems for your customer, not yourself.

CHAPTER 5

FOSTER A CREATIVE ENVIRONMENT

CREATIVITY IS A NATURAL PART OF THE HUMAN CONDITION. IMAG-ination is innate. Together, imagination and creativity lead to wonderful innovations. Innovations and connections that come out of left field, but when harnessed properly can be invaluable to businesses operating in a rapidly changing and disruptive environment. Unfortunately, most of us have had the imagination and creativity that we were born with beaten out of us – through our education, through the need to get by in a harsh world, and through our many responsibilities. It's still there, however. It just needs to be re-ignited. If you want your employees and partners to become more creative and imaginative, you need to provide them with an environment that helps them to reconnect with these natural qualities.

WHAT IS CREATIVITY?

Creativity is a way of understanding, a way of bending your mind to better grasp the world. Artistic pursuits such as painting, playing an instrument or writing are all forms of creativity. They are all similar in the sense that they connect concepts and bring them to life.

But creativity is not the sole preserve of artists such as painters, sculptors, or even songwriters and singers. Creativity rests in everyone – in all industries, in all vocations. Scientists and mathematicians can also be creative, not from an artistic perspective, but in terms of how they look at a problem and how they go about solving it. An entrepreneur who finds a new way of solving a problem for their customer is being creative.

Typically, when an idea is formed, it's not new; it might simply be the way in which we create new combinations of certain relationships. Being creative allows us to disconnect from our preconceived perceptions, and connections, and allows us to explore relationships and connections that create value. Identifying these relationships and connections also enables us to remove obstacles.

When you are being creative, you are looking at problems from a completely different angle. Often you are drawing upon different situations and learnings and understanding how it all connects. This is different from the way we think when we're being strictly rational. When we are attempting to think rationally, we are succumbing to the necessary shortcuts that our brain takes in order to be efficient.

Being creative allows you to open your mind to new possibilities, which are not bound by history or bias. It is one of the reasons why diversity is so valuable, because it provides new perspectives and new understandings that can be merged or connected with existing ones.

The mind is a very powerful organ in that it works to be as efficient as possible, but when you release the shackles the imagination can take you anywhere.

THE POWER OF RANDOM CONNECTIONS

The power of creativity in business can rely on random connections that are unlikely to occur in an efficient, buttoned-down business environment. As an example of how powerful creativity can be when people are allowed to pursue their interests freely and without a narrow focus, let's look at Steve Jobs dropping out of college but 'dropping in' on calligraphy classes. He talked about this in his Stanford Commencement Address:

> 'I decided to take a calligraphy class to [learn calligraphy]. I learned about serif and sans-serif typefaces, about varying the space between different letter combinations, about what makes great typography great. It was beautiful. Historical. Artistically subtle in a way that science can't capture. And I found it fascinating. None of this had any hope of any practical application in my life. But ten years later, when we were designing the first Macintosh computer, it all came back to me. And we designed it all into the Mac. It was the first computer with beautiful typography. If I had never dropped in on that single course in college, the Mac would never have had multiple typefaces or proportionally spaced fonts. And since Windows just copied the Mac, it's likely that no personal computer would have them.'

Or you could think of Mark Zuckerberg, who founded Facebook. Zuckerberg was a psychology major, although he took mainly computer science classes. If you think of Facebook, it merges these two disciplines beautifully. Through psychology, Zuckerberg understood the value of personal connection and relationships. He understood how society operated and that people have a desire to share, be connected, be part of a group and be able to communicate. The creative process led him to link that with computer science and develop a social network. Facebook would not have happened without the unlikely partnership of psychology and computer science.

But it can be hard to see how random connections can create an innovative and profitable solution in the future. Steve Jobs pointed out that: '*You can't connect the dots looking forward; you can only connect them looking backwards. So, you must trust that the dots will somehow connect in your future. You must trust in something – your gut, destiny, life, karma, whatever. This approach has never let me down, and it has made all the difference in my life.*'

When Steve Jobs took his calligraphy class, he never envisaged the level of impact that it would have on his business. He said himself that he did not believe it to have any practical application in his life, yet, it was most likely the master addition to his products that made Apple so successful. Mark Zuckerberg would have had next to no idea that taking psychology and computer science classes at the same time would lead him to where he is today. He was only able to connect the dots looking back.

So, how do we apply these lessons in our businesses? How do we foster creativity and imagination and connect these random dots? We need to do some reverse engineering. We need to understand how and why the natural creativity we had in childhood was beaten out of us, and find a way to let it re-emerge.

THE PROBLEM OF IMAGINATION

I remember when my son started school and I received a phone call from his teacher. He explained that we had a big problem and that my son was a liar. I was horrified, but quizzed the teacher to understand. He told me that my son, in show and tell, told the class that he was born in Africa and used to roam with wild animals like lions and elephants.

I said to the teacher that we did not have a problem; what we had was an imagination.

Society has a funny way of beating imagination out of us; my son was having the imagination beaten out of him when he was five years old by his first teacher. It also has a funny way of stopping us from playing the way we did when we were children.

It is well documented that as we get older, we lose the ability to play. We are conditioned to quickly filter information and make subconscious decisions based on a play book we have created in our minds. Which is fine; we need these shortcuts, otherwise we would be paralysed by indecision. This is set to serve us, particularly when life is busy. We don't have all day to examine and pull something apart. We often don't have the time to ask 'Why?' a hundred times, and we are probably too embarrassed to trial, draw or prototype a crazy idea for fear of social judgement.

But play allows for creativity. We need to play to progress. Sometimes our own intellect gets in our road, and as adults we tend to overthink or overanalyse problems. This is most likely why our best ideas come to us when we're in the shower or on holidays, because this is when our minds finally have a little space where we can think. But when do we get to explore those ideas further? If adults are always at or above capacity, where is the time to look for better ways to think, to explore, to test or to learn?

Of course, play needs some boundaries. We won't allow children to play in the middle of the street, nor will we allow them to play with knives or fire – safe environments and parameters must be created. But where is the safe place for adults? Where things can be broken down, where we can explore, perhaps fail, or perhaps come up with a truly brilliant solution to a problem that will pay for itself one hundred times over. This is the sort of environment we need to create in our organisations so that we can harness creativity and imagination and use it to innovate.

CREATE A PLAY PEN

When people can explore the creative aspect of problem identification and problem solving, they will come up with some very inspirational ideas, but we don't know when or how those moments will come. So we have to keep curating, keep supporting, keep providing the space, and provide leadership and frameworks so that when that moment comes, it can be nurtured. Ideas come from the most obscure of places, but they need an environment that has been geared to allow that to happen.

Creativity is not a single event, it is an ongoing event, so you want people to be creative every day, not just at the point that management deems it is now important to be creative. You can't force creativity or expect an idea to drop on demand, but what you can do is set up an environment that allows people creative space and tools, and encourages them to look for opportunity to frame problems and to be curious about finding better ways of doing things.

The ideas will then just come, and it does not matter if those ideas pop into our head during the night, on the drive to work, or mid conversation with someone. What is important is that you have trained the mind to be ready to pounce on the idea when it is seeded, and then allow that idea to come to life rather than just remain a wonderful, yet worthless, thought bubble. The space needs to be provided to harness these thought bubbles.

It's also important to keep people excited about entering the creative process; don't make it a burden for them. You must be very careful that you don't apply so much pressure on coming up with a creative moment that you destroy the ability to get there. You don't know when a child will take their first steps or utter their first words, but you do know that it will happen, and you will recognise when they are on the cusp of making that breakthrough. It is at that point that it is most critical to provide all the necessary support and be as patient as possible. It's about allowing what is going to happen to happen, and in a way that is not forced or pressured.

Once the breakthrough happens, the momentum will grow from that point – more steps, faster steps, or more words, sentences and conversations. It's the same with your business – you need to be patient and let the ideas germinate. There will, of course, be quick wins and other progress along the way. You generally get what you focus on, so if you are focused on improving or innovating your business, it will be very hard to prevent that from happening.

It's also important to protect your staff from unnecessary worry if you want them to be more creative, because one sure way to kill off creativity is to worry. Worrying about the next email coming in, worrying about time, worrying about meeting a day-to-day operational requirement, worrying about the next meeting, worrying about the financial review that will soon take place. Worry, worry, worry.

If your business is not well organised, if your staff fail to support each other, if there is a toxic culture, or if resources are stretched to the limit, your staff will be preoccupied with solving their immediate difficulties. Your team cannot become playful, imaginative, future-focused creative types in an environment like this. So, give them a well-run company and an optimistic environment so that they can put aside any worries they may have.

Creativity can be particularly challenging for operational and frontline staff, who are very much in the here and the now, the day to day, the moment. They cannot be distracted for too long, otherwise they may disappoint a customer, have service fail or place too much pressure on their colleagues to pick up the slack. They need the space, and potentially the permission, to contribute to the innovation and improvement of your organisation.

For this reason, it's a good idea to schedule workshops, seminars and training programs where your frontline staff can be taken out of their everyday environment and separated from operational concerns. When planned, scheduled and resourced appropriately, you will find that the benefits of doing this will be astounding. There will be an immediate payback of whatever investment you have made in embedding creativity as part of your organisation's systems, processes and culture. An example of this type of scheduled opportunity for creativity is Google's policy of allowing engineers to spend twenty per cent of their working week on projects that interest them personally. This is a great way of encouraging employees to explore their own ideas and bring new services and products to the company.

The following points are some of the ways you can help develop a creative capability:

- Focus on the first attribute in the Fit for Disruption model, being Commercial, to set a foundational mindset;
- Effectively manage workload and flows so that team members are efficiently utilised, but not overburdened;
- Have work environments established that are conducive to innovative and creative thinking – open plan, colourful;
- Have well organised and clean workspaces;
- Don't bombard the organisation with administration work – let the administrators do that, and let your operators operate;
- Break down the hierarchical barriers in your organisation – let information and feedback flow freely, regardless of title or position;
- Encourage team members to go and see what other companies and industries are doing;
- Encourage team members to network extensively so that a broad perspective is facilitated; and
- Where appropriate, give your people exposure to the entire organisation – don't be shy to move people between functions, even if it means spending some time in an area that is not their main discipline.

Fostering imagination and creativity in your organisation is important if you want your staff to be able to innovate. While some structure can be provided around this, it is more a matter of creating the right environment. It is one of those situations where you will have to let the future look after itself, and all you can do is give it the very best opportunity to succeed. Some won't have the patience for this, but this will be at their own peril, because if you are not innovating or improving your business, then your future will be bleak. Having that resilience, patience and confidence will pay dividends. Doing this in a continuous cycle will mean you are always delivering value, and the need for patience will be a thing of the past.

The first step in learning to Create is to build an environment that fosters imagination and creativity.

Your organisation needs to have the space and environment to be able to identify opportunities, find problems and work out how to solve them in simple and creative ways. If your team are stressed and always working at full capacity, they will never be in a position to be able to help add value, and they are likely to be stuck in a circular trap of knowing how to do things better but not being able to work on actually making things better. Your team need a broad perspective both inside and outside your business, and inside and outside your industry.

WHAT YOU CAN DO

☑ Ensure your environments are conducive to creativity and collaboration by introducing colour, removing clutter and abolishing physical barriers;

☑ Send your people to new environments, such as other players in the industry or other geographies, to give them a sense of what is possible, what best practice looks like, or what is already out there that can be adopted in your environment;

☑ Provide flexibility and time for your team to be able to work on individual projects; and

☑ Review your resource plans to ensure that your team have the capacity to execute business as usual, land new initiatives and develop new solutions.

CHAPTER 6

DEVELOP A CREATIVE MINDSET

PROVIDING A WORKING ENVIRONMENT THAT LETS PEOPLE REDIS-cover their creativity and imagination is essential if you want your organisation to be able to continuously innovate and improve. But it's also important that, once ideas have begun to emerge, they are supported and nurtured into fully fledged, value-adding products and services. In business, it's all too easy to dismiss ideas as impractical, too expensive or too crazy. But part of being creative is having the vision and courage to see where these ideas might take you. And that is all about having the right mindset.

OPEN YOUR MIND

If you want to remain profitable in a rapidly changing, disruptive business environment, you need to be innovative. That much is clear. But if you are going to innovate, you need to be open-minded. It is an essential step in being creative.

Our minds are littered with bias, preconceived ideas and fear. The problem with this is that it limits our mindset and creates ingrained patterns of thinking. There are times when this pattern of thinking serves us well. We need to be efficient in how we process information and get through the day. If our minds were always totally open, we would never get anything done. In the hustle and bustle of daily operations, however, it is almost impossible to find the space to be able to get off the treadmill and open your mind to new possibilities.

But it *is* possible to develop an open-mind capability within an organisation. Often it is simply creating awareness and giving people the breathing space to be able to have a clear head. When you start to look for opportunities, you will start to find them. It's like when you buy a new car – you start to see the car you want everywhere. Your awareness has been heightened and tuned into a specific purpose. It's the same with innovation; if the people in your organisation deliberately look for opportunity, they are more likely to find it.

Being prepared to explore new boundaries and to make seemingly unrelated connections can only serve an organisation. Curious minds uncover patterns, trends and associations. This curiosity and exploration delivers better thinking, a greater capacity to solve problems and more innovative ways to create value.

Ideas can come from anywhere. Look to see what other companies and other industries are doing. Explore the state of your industry in other countries, other sites or other departments. What is critical in this process is that effort needs to be made to go and explore with purpose. Be deliberate and curious and bring as much awareness as you possibly can.

Diversity is a powerful tool for opening minds. It brings so many perspectives, experiences and learnings to the table, and when these are shared it creates mutual respect and understanding. This is why travel is one of the best forms of education, because it opens the mind to new situations in different environments, and the appreciation of different ways to solve problems.

A sure-fire way to open the minds of your people is to provide a safe and collaborative environment where they can challenge the status quo, communicate new ideas and question assumptions. Being able to challenge requires a level of bravery, but the great organisations encourage and invite this level of constructive involvement. The organisations that do this poorly lose good people, or simply do not progress because people become focused on their own needs rather than the needs of the organisation.

BE BOLD

If you're going to be a creative organisation, you can't be shy. To create new solutions to old and new problems, we need to be bold. This is about embracing failure, building momentum, and having the confidence to put new ideas on the table. It is standing up and speaking the words that need to be said or breaking through stereo-types and refusing to accept the status quo.

Being bold is about challenging why things are done and how things are done. It is not about accepting history or 'the way things are done around here'. While history and context are clearly important, boldness will be what creates future value.

There is creative value in allowing people to speak their truth or speak the truth of the company – to call out the 'elephant in the room'. In an open and transparent environment, problems can be dealt with and solutions created.

Too often the leadership of an organisation might claim to be behind an innovative solution, but their actions are actually debilitating the process. Employees need to be bold to call it out. And they need to feel safe and secure in doing so. An organisation might believe that they are cutting edge in their industry, despite data that shows the opposite. In an environment that encourages its people to be bold, they will have the courage to challenge that and show that the organisation has started to believe its own rhetoric.

Having an environment where truth can be spoken, appropriately and respectfully, means that awareness is created. If the truth cannot be spoken and voices are stifled, no creative solutions can be offered. How many times have we heard the saying: 'Nobody listens around here' or 'We can't talk about that' or 'We can't challenge the boss'?

Older generations are perhaps less likely to challenge the status quo in this way, as they're accustomed to hierarchies in companies where they essentially 'run ideas up the flagpole'. Elon Musk sees it differently and says in his communication policy: *'Anyone at Tesla can and should email/talk to anyone else according to what they think is the fastest way to solve a problem for the benefit of the whole company.'*

Being bold is a mindset of possibility, not probability. It is open and more aware of new opportunities for creating value. Being bold will lead to finding reasons why something *can* be done, not why it *can't*. It is also about showing vulnerability, which not only helps build empathy, but also fosters an open and transparent environment. It demonstrates that everyone makes mistakes, but that everyone can also learn from them. It helps overcome fears and builds a community around problem solving.

Having the courage to be an individual, to express one's own worth, becomes empowering. Creating this safe environment builds further trust and becomes contagious. If you have an organisation that values being bold and is motivated by demonstrating courage, it will be able to face the new era with confidence and be able to redefine how things are done.

A closing point on being bold. The most successful company I have ever worked at has being bold as one of their values. As does Facebook, which is one of the most successful and influential companies of this era. Both these organisations accept that they will not always get it right and mistakes will be made. But they both have a fundamental belief that the biggest risk is to take no risks at all.

THINK ABUNDANT AND RESOURCEFUL

Having a mindset focused on abundance and resourcefulness is essential in supporting your creativity. Thinking in terms of abundance creates a positive mindset, where all the possibilities are on the table and all situations are viewed as opportunities. Having an abundant mindset broadens the thinking in terms of what can be done and how it will come. It will lead to new ideas, creations and innovations because limits are not placed on possibilities, and the collective mind can ponder new and exciting ways to solve problems and to create value.

Resourcefulness is also an important mindset to have. Being resourceful allows teams to establish very creative and innovative ways to make something happen and get it done without wasting resources. In this sense, resourcefulness also supports the business to be commercial.

If the mindset is not an abundant one, teams will just see problems and obstacles. They will be slow to respond, and not solve problems effectively. Not being resourceful will lead to high levels of waste and will also take resources away from areas that need them.

Having a mindset focused on abundance and resourcefulness is a skill, and it is a key organisational capability that will be required to succeed in disruptive environments. Fortunately, it can be acquired – it just means reframing your thinking.

Earlier in my career I was speaking with an executive about my resource challenges. He asked me how many people I had working for me, and from memory I just placed a number on the amount of direct reports I had at the time. He told me that was rubbish. He said that everyone worked for me: he worked for me, every employee of the organisation worked for me, the suppliers and service providers worked for me, even the leadership worked for me. He said I needed to pretend I was the CEO and think that all the resources were available to me – I just had to articulate why I needed them, and engage whom I needed to help me with what I was trying to achieve. It was a good lesson; he was teaching me how to be resourceful and not to place limitations on my thinking.

There will always be resource constraints, no matter what organisation you work with, work for, or maybe even found. So having a resourceful and abundant mindset is critical if you're going to be creative, and also to support commercial performance.

We can look at this another way, too. Let me ask you something: How many of the top 100 companies of ten years ago still make that list? How many have lost their dominant position? It does not matter which list you reference; the fact is that the dominant companies of ten years ago are dying and new companies that have led innovation now monopolise these lists – think Amazon, Apple, Facebook, Google, Uber, LinkedIn. But how can that be? Surely the leading companies had the most resources. Of course they did. So, the reason that they are dying and new stars are rising is surely the mindset that these groups have around resourcefulness or scarcity.

The right mindset is often found in new, modern companies. People are leaving traditional organisations in droves because they are not able to develop ideas. People believe that they have more chance – so, in essence, more resource – to do this on their own than in a corporate environment. Remember that starting and operating a business on a global scale is now accessible to anyone in the world who possesses a laptop and mobile device. The corporate world should harness this intellect and passion, not push these innovators out the door so that they can go and create something that will make the organisation they once worked for redundant.

Your organisation, no matter how big or small, is under threat. That statement is now as sure as death and taxes. If your organisation fails to think differently about abundance, it will be in for a struggle. At least the pain will be quick – because innovative companies, big and small, are starting to dominate and the momentum has only just started.

TRUST YOUR INSTINCTS

It is wise to seek information, opinions and counsel, particularly from people who are experts in their field. We must always have an open mind and be willing to listen. This is part of learning, and if we didn't have the humility to listen then we would be in some trouble.

However, you must also know when to stop seeking opinions, when to stop listening, and when to have confidence and believe in yourself. If the experts had all the answers, they would already have changed, innovated or disrupted what it is you are working on. When you're looking for innovative, new solutions to problems –whether those problems are old or new – you need to trust that you will find them, and that your instincts are right.

People around you often get it wrong or are less than encouraging – not necessarily maliciously, but because they lack vision or foresight. In 1995 a famous article published by Clifford Stroll basically said the internet was all hype. We must also remember that our brains are wired to identify threats – whatever form they take – and innovations can be seen as threats, especially by people who think their job will be put in jeopardy by coming changes. So of course they will try to discourage you.

Often the experts have a sense of ownership and connection to the old way of doing things that will simply not allow them to see past their own perspective. They also may be protective of their space, as it is their reputation, their ego and potentially their livelihood that you are challenging with your new ideas. And while you may think you are coming at it with good intentions, they may feel threatened.

And sometimes it can be more sinister. Some experts may be nice to your face, but undermine you through wrong information, misinformation, miscommunication, or simply by not being open about what you can do. I once worked on a major project where the program was being stonewalled by a senior leader – not because the program did not have merit, but because this leader believed that that it would highlight his incompetency and failings.

So, while it's important to listen to the experts, you should be aware of both their motives and natural limitations and understand how those factors can influence the advice they give you. Ultimately, you must make up your own mind and be brave enough to trust your instincts.

The second step in learning to Create is to develop the right mindset.

Unfortunately, many businesses are limited in their thinking around how to solve a problem in an effective manner. A creative business will develop open-mindedness as a business capability.

WHAT YOU CAN DO

☑ Be bold and open your mind. Step out of your comfort zone. Identify the deep-seated assumptions of the organisation and challenge them, then take immediate action to change those that are outdated;

☑ Do not accept a culture that will not allow honesty and freedom of expression – get every issue out into the open;

☑ Bring attention to what resources are available to your organisation – beyond financial resources. Teach your organisation how to look for resourceful ways of solving problems;

☑ Don't be wishy washy – get real and focused on your innovation strategy and direction; just start with a resourceful and abundant mindset; and

☑ Learn to respect experts, but don't place them on a pedestal and do listen to your own instincts.

CHAPTER 7

PICK A PROBLEM

THE BEST WAY TO BE SUCCESSFUL IN A DISRUPTIVE ENVIRONMENT is to create solutions to previously unsolved problems. This is the second attribute of the Fit for Disruption model. You need to build an environment that fosters creativity and embrace a mindset that supports the ideas that this environment is designed to create. Once you have these ideas and innovations, you must find a problem to solve. And you should solve problems not for yourself, but for your customers.

One of the great things about problems is that they often seem really complicated, however, with leadership, teamwork and some simple methods, the task of problem solving can become a significant advantage for you – in terms of both the problems you solve and the speed at which you can do it.

PROBLEMS ARE A GOOD THING

If you're in business, you're in the business of solving problems. Businesses are engaged in trade, the commercial exchange of goods and services, where the objective is to profit from the trade transactions.

On the demand side we have a problem; on the supply side we should have a solution. You can come up with the most incredible product or service, but if it does not solve a problem there will be no demand for the solution.

The world has many problems. For those of us lucky enough to live in a first-world country, our problems may be as superficial as what car we drive, the thread count of our cotton sheets or which mobile telephone plan we should have. In the developing world, problems can be much more serious.

Rich countries, poor countries, all demographics, all sectors of society are experiencing problems. There are old problems that are becoming bigger, such as how to feed ourselves as populations grow and we compete for food resources on a global scale.

We also have new problems. An ageing population, climate change, the onset of digital connectivity, and the emergence of China and Asia in the political and economic landscape are creating new worries. Even the fact that people now prefer to buy experiences, not things, is creating a problem for traditional businesses.

The issue will not be finding a problem and solution to it – that will be the easy part. The issue will be deciding which problem to solve first; that is, which problem is most important to your business and to your stakeholders and which solution will provide the most value.

It's easy to run off on tangents and shift focus from what is trying to be achieved at a strategic level. You need to focus on the right problems – ones that mean something to your business. If you can persevere with a difficult problem, the rewards should be plentiful.

But if the problem is too hard to solve, find another one – there is no shortage.

So how should we decide which problems to solve? The key here is understanding your customers and defining their problems.

CONNECT WITH YOUR CUSTOMERS

Before you create a solution to a problem, you need to know what the problem is. This starts by understanding your customers' experience. Ultimately, it's the customers' problems that you should be solving. This is why you're in business. To understand your customers' problems, you need to understand their whole experience.

The customer experience begins well before they even know that your organisation exists; it starts when they realise they have a problem that needs solving. This could be needing a new outfit to attend a party or wanting a meal in a hurry when they arrive home late, or they might need to find a better insurance premium.

Understanding the mindset and conditions of the people you are creating solutions for helps frame problems from their perspective, not your own. You get to understand their pain points and develop a greater appreciation of what matters to them. But understanding is not a theoretical desktop exercise; it involves deeply immersing yourself in every aspect of your customer's situation. Feeling it first-hand provides an appreciation of the underlying issues and emotions, the root causes and the anomalies that come into play. Through immersion you gain context, and context will provide the power to create ideas and solutions that will have significance. It will help you to distinguish between your customers' physical needs, such as needing a hammer to punch a nail into a wall, and their emotional needs, such as needing to hang a portrait of their beloved great aunt to remember and honour her after her passing.

Having this level of understanding means that the business can focus on whom they are solving problems for and why they are solving them, and ensure that they are best placed to solve the problem. This will help prioritise resource and effort, while minimising distraction.

Often businesses go about developing products, services and solutions that do not meet any of their customers' needs. They may touch on the superficial need, but not the real emotional need that is at the heart of the problem. Profitable businesses will not make this mistake. They will see that there is significant value to be unlocked by understanding unmet needs and how they can be resolved. And these unmet needs can only be identified by empathising deeply with your customers' situation.

It is basic psychology that we all have this feeling of needing to be understood. When you have that moment of understanding, you are connected and the trust builds. Your ideas will become more accepted; your audience will also be able to respect your guidance and counsel and will be more open to change.

So, let's look at a couple of structured methods for understanding your customers.

Develop an empathy map
You can map out the customer or stakeholder journey and timeline

by creating an empathy map. When deciding what to include in the map, focus on:

- **Quotes and defining words** heard during observations and conversations.
- **Thoughts and beliefs** of the customers or stakeholders you speak with. E.g. 'This will never change' or 'If we don't do x, y can't happen'.
- **Actions, behaviours and routines** of the people you observe, such as the steps they take, process they follow, tone and body language they exhibit.
- **Feelings and emotions** at each critical point. The emotions they are experiencing – such as frustration when attempting to communicate with someone, or delight when they receive an online order in full and on time.

EMPATHY MAP

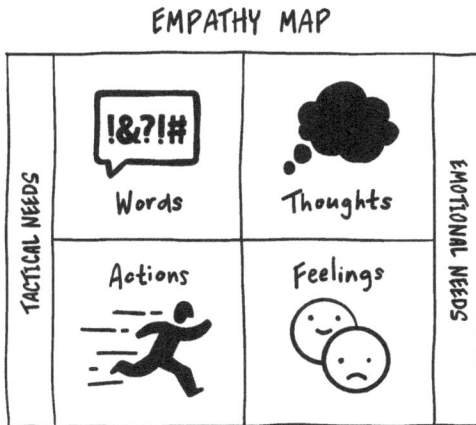

Following from the empathy map, you can then draw a map that illustrates the journey your customer goes on, showing when and where a need arises, an activity takes place, emotions are felt or a need is met.

CUSTOMER JOURNEY MAP

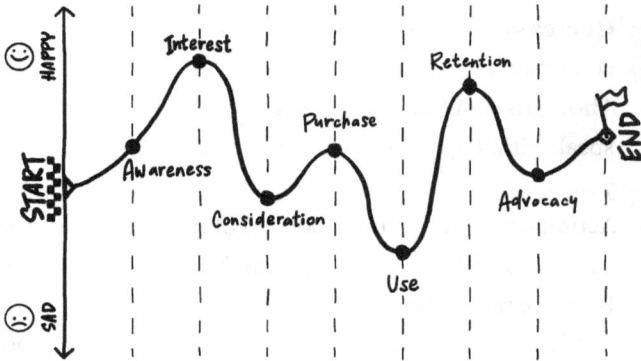

GIVE THE CUSTOMERS WHAT THEY NEED

Solving customers' problems and creating a valuable experience for them goes beyond simply asking them what they want. In fact, asking them what they want can be counterproductive. Henry Ford once said, '*If I had asked people what they wanted, they would have said faster horses.*' Steve Jobs said that: '*Customers do not know what they want until you show them.*'

If you simply react to a customer's request, you may lose an opportunity to be creative. While it may appear that both Henry Ford and Steve Jobs pushed products down the line, the reality is that they both had a great sense of what the customers' problems were and could empathise with them and come up with completely new and innovative ways of resolving their problems. Ford and Jobs would have studied the problem, observed customers and how they went about their business, and understood at a deep level how to resolve their problems.

While your customers do not need to come up with all the ideas, they can help you define the problem and understand how the problem impacts them. Once you identify a solution, your customer should be given a chance to be engaged in the process of testing and learning. See how your customer behaves with the proposed solution and allow them to interact with the solution and experience whatever emotions come to them. This can help you improve on your idea. Your customers may get a lightbulb moment that you can incorporate into your idea and come up with an end solution that is far superior. If the customer feels like they have been part of developing the solution, they are also much more likely to embrace the finished solution.

Carefully considering your customers' need will help you to keep their problems in perspective. Often people try to over-spec a solution beyond what is needed. It is like having a Formula 1 car for driving around suburban streets – it's not at all practical, you could never get the value out of its performance capability, and you would have nowhere to store your groceries. You do not have to crack a nut with a sledgehammer; it is important to keep everything in perspective in the value-creation process. It's also possible that your customers think they know what they need and think that the products they're currently using suit them perfectly. They may be very attached to a product or service, but you must be prepared to destroy something that you know customers do, in fact, value. Let me explain.

Being attached to an idea, product or business that has lost its relevance in the market is one way to impede your business performance. This sometimes means letting go, and sometimes that may be a big part of your business. Kodak, Blockbuster and Borders are all examples of companies that should have considered cannibalising their own products.

Apple is a company that knows how to do this. The iPhone has all the capabilities that the iPod had, and the iPod is now redundant. In fact, the iPhone was launched when iPod sales were still going through the roof. But Steve Jobs believed that if there was a better way of doing something, you must find it and produce it. He reportedly said, '*If you don't cannibalise your own products, someone else will.*'

Many organisations have not survived because they have failed to let go of a model or product that is no longer relevant. They spend an exorbitant amount of energy and resource trying to prop up the failing offer, and it ultimately sucks the life out of the entire organisation. If it must die, let it die gracefully and avoid your own Kodak moment. By creating offers that are more relevant to a changing market, you will have an opportunity to redefine your organisation, and buffer the impact of the dying offer.

LEARN TO FOCUS

> '*People think focus means saying yes to the thing you've got to focus on. But that's not what it means at all. It means saying no to the hundred other good ideas that there are. You must pick carefully. I'm actually as proud of the things we haven't done as the things I have done. Innovation is saying no to 1,000 things.*'
> STEVE JOBS

Imagine the power created by being completely focused, without distraction or interference. Your ability to think, solve problems and create will reach a level that breaks through barriers.

While saying yes feels good and implies cooperation and teamwork, saying yes to too many things, or the wrong thing, may in fact be stifling your progress and ability to succeed. Saying no is difficult, whether you have to say it to a teammate, a customer or someone in your personal life. However, we simply cannot be all things to all people, and we need to focus our efforts where they will have the most impact. If you don't, you will be letting your team down because you have been unable to deliver the success that you otherwise could have if you focused properly. And that in itself is a type of no.

You need to be able to prioritise the ideas that come in and choose the right ones to execute. You don't want to jump on every new, shiny, bright light, and there is no point executing well on things that will have little impact on your organisation. The ideas either need to fit into your strategy or be so compelling that they make a change of course worthwhile. Remember the principles of being commercial at this stage; they are critically important in the assessment and prioritisation process. Focus your strategy and stick to it. Be very good at what you do, and aim your sniper gun, not your scatter gun.

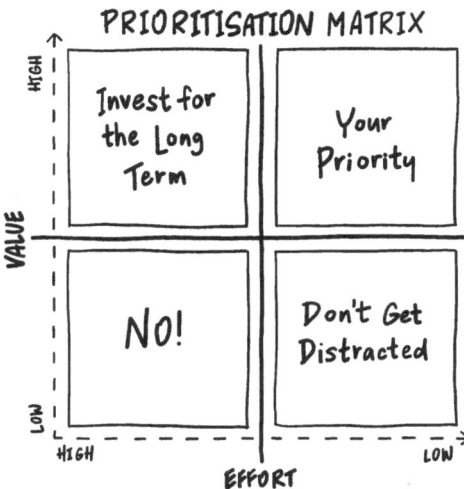

PRIORITISATION MATRIX

	HIGH	LOW
HIGH	Invest for the Long Term	Your Priority
LOW	NO!	Don't Get Distracted

VALUE — EFFORT

DON'T REINVENT THE WHEEL

When deciding where to focus, you should also remember that you don't have to reinvent the wheel. There is so much out there that can be improved, which means that you don't always have to start from scratch when finding a solution to a problem. The idea is to continuously improve on the product, service or process – not necessarily reinvent it.

Of course, this is not to say that if you come up with a brilliant first-time product, service or operational improvement that you shouldn't back yourself on it – to the contrary. However, for ninety-nine per cent of the problems out there, the solution is likely to already exist in another shape of form – it just needs to be modified, developed and taken to the next level.

For operational improvements, it may even be as simple as looking to see who does it well. When I was running an operational improvement program for a large retailer, the first thing I did was look across the network of over 200 stores to see who did the operation well and what could be learned. I also looked at the poor operations, as this provided insight into what could go wrong and why. I then scanned other retailers from across the globe to get an inside look at how they were approaching the same problem. Next, I looked at other industries to see how they approached similar issues – for instance, how did the airlines manage queues, how did McDonalds manage service, how did Apple build design features into its product?

Great solutions to problems may be out there already in another form if you open your mind and take notice or have the opportunity to experiment.

CREATE VALUE FOR ALL

So far, we've been talking about giving the customer what they want, but you need to do this without taking value away from the organisation. There must be value for all.

The modern-day customer loves to be made to feel special and unique. They also want clear choices. The customer wants their individual needs and problems met; they do not want to have to fit into a box and compromise their individuality or their needs. They want a personalised experience.

On the other hand, organisations like to build in standardisation so that they can get efficiencies of scale, and so that their processes become replicable and easily trained. This not only helps keep costs down, it also aids predictability in terms of quality, service outcomes and availability. Although they might not realise it, standardisation adds value for the customer.

If we think about what the overall objectives are, it's really about being able to provide the best customer experience in a commercially viable way. The good news is that personalisation and standardisation can absolutely coexist. In many instances, it is the standardisation that can provide the ability to customise because it sets a structural base from which the innovation can build.

Take IKEA. You can absolutely shop their store and bring your own personality to the purchases that you make. You can select colours, styles, size, accessories, even comfort levels. It was not that long ago that I went into an IKEA store and created a set of custom wardrobes based upon certain requirements in terms of size and finish, and the number of shelves and railings. I was able to choose sliding doors over front-opening doors and a glossy, white finish, and ensure that there were allocated spaces and specific drawers for my wife's shoes.

This personalisation was made possible by the fact that the IKEA furniture is standardised in terms of its design, manufacturing and even packaging. It was like playing with Lego, and I just mixed and matched standard products to achieve a personalised outcome.

Personalisation and standardisation need to be in your thinking as you go about the Create phase.

It's also important not to try to be all things to all people. Often organisations go about innovation by reacting and responding to the stimuli of the day. This can lead them to be sympathetic to all the customers' issues and concerns but, instead of defining problems and identifying value-creating solutions that benefit all parties, they go about changing or creating things that bring no value to the organisation. The whole objective of innovation is to create value for all, not diminish value within your own organisation for the sake of your customers' every whim.

The third step in learning to Create
is to develop problem identification
and solving capabilities.

Understanding the customer journey will help you understand the pain that they feel, and the problems that they need solved. Emotions are a very big part of the customer decision-making process, and it is imperative that these emotional impacts are considered in the identification of problems and development of solutions. By better understanding the customers' needs, and unmet needs, the greater opportunity you have to develop solutions that will add real value.

WHAT YOU CAN DO

- ☑ Learn about and observe your customers and the environments that they operate in. Collect data and key information. Become immersed in the environment and ensure that leaders, managers and operators gain these perspectives;
- ☑ Review all processes, products and services and determine their contribution to the value of the organisation and to the customer, with a view to stopping production of anything that does not add value;
- ☑ Identify areas of your organisation where you are potentially over-servicing or under-servicing a customer;
- ☑ Prepare a 'Stop Doing' list; and
- ☑ Determine where your organisation can standardise processes, and where they can add personalisation for the customer.

CHAPTER 8

LEARN BY DOING

IF YOU WANT TO CREATE INNOVATIVE SOLUTIONS AND MAKE A PROFIT in a disruptive, rapidly changing business environment, you need to learn by doing. You also need to learn to fail, as many small failures allow you to move quickly.

Learning equips us to solve problems, to identify issues, to execute a task or process as expected. It helps us have the confidence to question the status quo, to think of different ways to solve problems, even to identify the problems themselves. You want your organisation to be able to become skilled at creating, acquiring, transferring and developing knowledge and insights that support the growth of the organisation and the creation of opportunity, empathy and resilience. Without a learning environment, change becomes cosmetic and ultimately unsustainable.

Learning can be designing; it may be experimenting. You want your organisation to be able to learn from others, to have diverse perspectives and impacts. You will need structured learning and some unstructured learning, there will be some classroom learning, and there should be a lot of on-the-job and practical training.

FAIL FAST, FAIL OFTEN AND WIN

I was very fortunate to once have a leader who, at performance review time, asked to discuss my failures. At that point I felt like I should collect my belongings and leave the building immediately. But he said that if I was not failing enough, I was not testing enough of my own boundaries, and that I could not be a future leader if I didn't know what it was like to fail properly. If you are failing the most, it means you are trying the most.

Profitable organisations are in the practice of conducting fast, cheap experiments to gain valuable insights and useful data points, and they are prepared to embrace failure as a form of learning. They learn by doing and are not waiting for perfection. This does not mean a compromise on quality; it just means that the sooner you can be in the market testing and learning, the better you will be. The market, customers and users will help you define the next steps. Take the iPhone, and the various iterations that have been produced since the first one was launched. They keep getting better and better, with each version based on learnings from the previous one.

Failing slow, on the other hand, is mostly fatal. When Woolworths Australia entered the hardware space in the Australian market to compete with the dominant and successful Bunnings, it created an AU$3.25 billion blunder. They went all in, locking in real estate deals, opening over sixty stores that were big box, large format retail setups, and creating a comprehensive product range. While hindsight is a wonderful thing, I can't help but wonder what would have happened if they had completed more trials, tested with the customer, and learned from smaller failures. Would they have learned that women did not want to shop at a fancy hardware store, that they liked the rough and ready style of Bunnings? Would they have learned that tradespeople did not feel the location or the environment helped them? Would they have learned that the range they offered made little sense to the customer? It was likely that they did have this information, but either it was too late to act on it or they just failed to learn or listen.

Remember, however, that you don't want to fail for failure's sake. It is not a concept to hide incompetence. When visiting a major start-up in Silicon Valley recently, one of the executives told me: 'Failure is success ONLY if you deep dive and learn from it.' In other words, learn by doing.

Short, quick, cheap experiments that fail pose insignificant risk and impact if managed and controlled properly. They provide a relatively safe way for participants to be bold and more creative in their thinking.

Given that no creative initiative follows a straight line from concept to realisation, the fail fast, fail often mantra provides the opportunity to pivot and adjust course depending on what is happening in the environment. It is easy to see the causal effects of a trial or pilot, establish what is working well, and accelerate or temper as the situation requires. It provides an early opportunity to cut losses on an idea and reduce exposure.

The value of the insights and feedback can be incorporated into the overall creation process and solution design. There is a constant cycle of collecting and building valuable data. The process is highly collaborative and engaging, so the process also helps build buy-in from the stakeholder community.

While prolific beats perfect, it is not an excuse to deliver poor performance and low-quality output. Prolific is about momentum and moving forward with frequent iterations. Prolific does not mean that anything less than your best effort is required, and it certainly does not mean that you can take shortcuts on quality. Each and every effort needs to build towards the goal.

The overall objective is clearly not to fail overall, but ultimately to win often and win more often than you fail. The benefits of all the wins must outweigh the failures. It is very difficult to value the failures – particularly at culture level, because there are so many intrinsic learning benefits that can be realised – but at a very basic level it is enough to say that the value of the wins must be greater than the failures. You can lose the battle, but you must win the war.

BE METHODICAL

It's important to have a process in place that can quickly assess the merits of the ideas that will start to come thick and fast when you turn your organisation's attention to innovation. Of course, not all ideas are going to be great ones, so it is important to have a process that justly considers all ideas and provides timely feedback, whether the idea is good or bad. The quickest way to shut down the innovation culture and stop generating ideas is to provide *no* feedback on an idea.

So, let's have a quick look at some methods for finding and testing innovative solutions to your customers' problems.

Design thinking

A modern and popular method is the Design Thinking approach, which is centred on the customer. It also acknowledges the emotional aspects of business, and the framework cleverly blends emotions with practical elements. This creates action and momentum.

The process of Design Thinking is nonlinear. There is no place to start or finish, the steps do not have to follow any specific order, and they often occur in parallel with each other. There is constant iteration, and returning to points in the process to enable refinement of ideas and concepts is intrinsic to the approach.

There are five universally accepted steps to Design Thinking;

1. **Empathise** – Understand the emotional journey of and impacts on the people you are designing a solution for.
2. **Define** – Articulate the problem and pain points experienced by the people you are designing a solution for.
3. **Ideate** – Generate out-of-the-box ideas that could address the problem as experienced by the people you are designing a solution for.
4. **Prototype** – Create.
5. **Test** – Solutions.

DESIGN THINKING

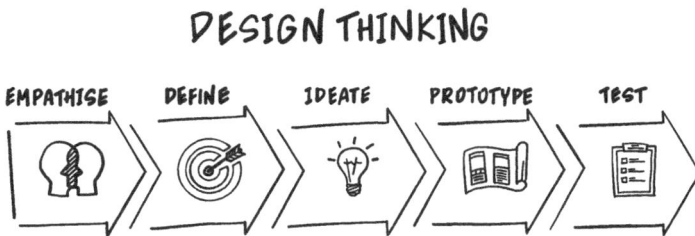

Plan, Do, Check, Act (PDCA)

PDCA is similar to Design Thinking, but also an effective problem-solving approach. It is useful in testing improvement measures on a small scale, and provides the ability to iterate, learn and continuously improve on an idea. The process is circular and includes solutions testing, analysing results and improving the process or concept.

1. **Plan** – Identify the problem
2. **Do** – Test potential solutions (creating prototypes)
3. **Check** – Study results (quantitative and qualitative)
4. **Act** – Implement the best solution and continuously improve

PLAN-DO-CHECK-ACT

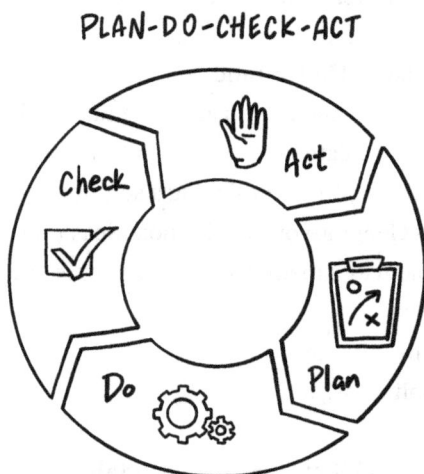

5 Ws and 1H

This is a problem-solving method that starts by identifying a problem, then breaks it into bite-size chunks and waits for themes to occur. Being able to see where all the relationships and connections are helps zone in on the problem. Ask:

- **Whom** does the problem affect, and whom does it benefit?
- **What** was the event, impact or action involved?
- **Where** did the problem occur?
- **When** did the problem occur – what are the time-related influences?
- **Why** did it happen? Identify the root cause.
  - To get to the root cause, use the 5 Whys approach – ask 'Why?' five times, with each answer forming the basis of the next question. This should establish the cause and effect relationships and help you understand the root cause of the problem, which in turn will help define the problem.
- **How** did events unfold?

Once you have identified and defined the problem correctly, you can use the 5Ws and 1H framework to express your proposed solution. Depending on how an opportunity presents, you can then ask how you can solve the problem commercially by adding value, understanding market or internal opportunities that will derive new revenue streams, and establishing the likely investments and cost structures that may be involved. You can then turn your hand to more detailed, solution-centred approaches, and so on.

Remember that these models are developed to guide you. They are not fixed or prescriptive – they are simply frameworks that organise and simplify an approach so that you can focus on the most important elements. While there will be critical elements you should not ignore, particularly around defining the problem correctly, you can mix and match any of the elements from any of the models as you see fit.

INNOVATION HUBS

Now that you've learned some methods for identifying problems and finding potential solutions, you need a place to practise these new skills. You need somewhere that you can learn by doing and fail creatively in a practical way. One of the best ways to do this is to use innovation hubs. They will be your soft place to fall, and most importantly your place to grow.

Innovation hubs are common spaces where communities and engagement can be built around your innovation. These hubs can call upon subject matter expertise, generate insight, enable discussion and knowledge transfer, or simply act as a place and forum for communication, sharing and collaboration around ideas and concepts.

The hub should be a place of collaboration and facilitation. It should be where all stakeholders can come and meet on neutral territory and learn, understand and contribute to the process. It should be a place of idea sharing and bold conversation. Each hub should allow decision makers to meet with operators and business subject experts to discuss complex business problems. The hubs should offer demonstrations of emerging solutions – such as technology or process improvement initiatives.

In a practical sense, innovation hubs do not need to be big and fancy or try to solve the most complex problems. Quite often an innovation hub is just a repurposed office or meeting room that provides a space to solve problems, ideate and develop prototypes. I have had these hubs created in the back rooms of stores or in allocated spaces in a distribution centre. I know of one very large financial institution that has a hub no bigger than a bedroom – yet, it is effective because it centres information, effort, communication and engagement. In fact, innovation hubs do not even need a fixed physical location – they can be transient.

There is no prescriptive requirement for the successful set-up of an innovation hub. The space and environment can be large, small, digital or simply a space with lots of Post-It notes.

Ideally, the innovation hub will be set up with all the key communications and outputs from any aspect of the design process. The hub should be full of examples of best practice and prototypes of what is possible. The hub should also visually demonstrate why there needs to be change and motivate people to become contributors themselves, or at least supporters.

It must also be collective and engaging. You want an environment where people feel that they can put their defences down and have a real conversation about what is possible and how to contribute.

By definition, an innovation hub is unique to the environment and organisation that creates it. It is designed for open experimentation, not rigidly following a list of prescribed routines or methods. While setting up an innovation hub will very much be a case of what is right for your environment, there will be some principles to follow. Each hub will:

- Seek to solve real problems;
- Be sited away from the distraction of day-to-day operational problems;
- Become a place where collaboration can occur;
- Provide an opportunity for stakeholders to participate, interact and learn;

- Facilitate prototyping; and
- Develop an ecosystem of contributors, partners, customers, experts, leaders and others who can quickly help accelerate and scale the innovation.

Innovation hubs are environments deliberately designed to bind together the organisation, strengthen it and deliver value.

Many of the biggest names in business are creating innovation hubs. No two innovation hubs are the same and they apply different methods and ask different questions to solve different problems. Some partner with technology companies to develop new apps and are isolated almost to the point of secrecy. Some are hackathons. Others provide a space for people to work on personal projects that help the company grow.

An example of a big innovation hub is the 'X –Moonshot factory', which was founded by Google to work on moonshots – radical new technologies to make the world a better place. Some of the problems they are working on include:

- How can balloons deliver the internet to rural and unconnected places? How can drones change the way goods are delivered around the world?
- How can kites be used to generate electricity in unexpected places?
- How can beams of light support the rapidly growing demand for data?

CENTRES OF LEARNING

Another very effective way to collaborate, engage and learn is to have a centre of learning, where deep interactions can take place with team members and customers. These centres allow for experimental learning. They can be used to identify and empathise with customers and team members, to define a problem and provide a real life setting to develop the ideas and concepts that will solve it. The benefit is that it's a live environment, not an ivory tower removed from reality.

The difference between an innovation hub and a centre for learning is that the centre for learning will be an actual operational setting – such as a store, a branch office, a distribution centre or a manufacturing plant (or line). An innovation hub may be more focused on product and new enterprises, whereas a centre for learning is an environment for innovation of the operational methods and ways of working.

The same principles apply to both, but a centre of learning also has the following elements:

- Assessment of impacts on customers and team members;
- The ability to work directly with customers and team members for innovation and improvement ideas;
- A focus on driving operational efficiency, productivity and service levels; and
- A way to determine impacts of upstream or head office decision making and processes.

Team members love being involved because it makes them feel like they are part of the bigger picture and take great pride in showcasing developments and refining solutions. It also creates an environment that sparks discussion and ideas that support the creative process.

You can trial different methods and solutions to problems and gain almost instantaneous feedback in a centre of learning. It is low risk. It supports the fail fast concept as you can quickly unwind any changes made in error.

The team members in these sites become the best advocates for innovation because they have experienced the change, are deeply engaged in developing the solutions, and are trained in making fast and agile decisions. You can invite other stakeholders to come and see the solution in action (or, in some centres, to see the problems in action).

As the centre of learning site matures and the process, technology or solution is bedded down, the site can then become a **centre of excellence**, which provides an example of what good looks like, and encapsulates all the leadership, best practice, research and support. These sites can then be used as training facilities, and, better still, you can have the operators and customers from the centre of excellence become the advocates for greater roll-out of and participation in the idea.

These centres of learning also act as enablers for acceleration of operational innovation. For example, I once set up a centre of learning in a large discount retailer. It took six months to effectively innovate and redesign the operational processes and ways of working. This was then rolled out to a further seven stores in various states to ensure that the new methods were scalable. This took approximately three months. Once the operational methods were proven, they were rolled out to the remaining fleet of approximately 185 stores in just six weeks.

This rapid rate of acceleration was possible for a number of reasons:

- We went slow to go fast;
- We were doing, not talking;
- The environment was real, not theoretical;
- Team members innovated the new methods and solutions, which lent them credibility with their peers in other stores;
- The team members owned the solution;
- Team members from other stores could come to the centres of learning to see exactly what the improvements and methods were;
- Team members could learn the new operating methods in a live environment, not in a classroom; and
- We were able to iron out any obvious flaws not only in the operating model, but also in the implementation of the model – we learned and iterated.

That particular initiative delivered tens of millions of dollars in ongoing benefit to the organisation – as well a massive uplift in morale and engagement.

> The fourth step in learning to Create is to start learning by doing.

The advantage lies in being able to act – prolific beats perfection. This is about testing ideas, building prototypes, soliciting feedback and establishing, very quickly, what works and what doesn't. Important data points, both qualitative and quantitative, are captured, and learnings are then built into the design at a rapid pace. The circular process continues and builds upon itself to create a solution that is user or customer-ready, and which has had customers' investment of ideas and trial inbuilt.

WHAT YOU CAN DO

☑ Build prototypes of your solutions in a fun workshop environment;

☑ Run small, controlled tests with the market, collecting valuable data, useful information and engagement observations;

☑ Have your organisation become competent in the understanding and application of problem-solving and idea-generating frameworks;

☑ Create an innovation hub, as large or small as you like, where people can collaborate, meet, communicate, develop and showcase; and

☑ Create a centre of learning – an operation (site, store, office, etc.) that can test and learn the solutions – providing opportunity for feedback, engagement, showcasing and training.

THE PRIZES OF BEING ABLE TO CREATE

The following embody the benefits of getting this attribute right:

New commercial solutions – new markets

As new ideas emerge and become user or customer-ready, value is created. This value will often be unique and something that either can't be replicated or opens new markets for domination. It becomes new revenue streams, new opportunities for team members, new ways to be able to contribute and add value. If nothing else, you will remain relevant.

Delighted customers

Your customers, new and old, will be delighted because you have solved their problems, because you have understood them. We all have an insatiable need to be understood, and when the customer feels understood and a solution is provided, value is created. These customers are happy to pay for value, and you are not locked in a price war.

A fun and engaging environment

You are creating an engaging and fun environment that people connect with. People can put their skills and creativity to use and feel valued in the process. Retention rates will soar, you will attract new talent, and your workplace will be a desirable place to be. The benefits will then compound, as the absence of stress and anxiety leads to greater creativity and better solutions.

Accelerating past the competition

New innovations that create value will deliver competitive advantage. You will have better methods and better solutions. You will be more relevant, and cheaper, faster and easier to do business with. You will generate loyalty and new customers will emerge. Instead of watching the competitors speed past you, you are speeding past them and opening new space that is unavailable to anyone else.

Impact

Having the ability to make an impact, to leave a legacy or to create something that has significant meaning beyond a commercial objective is priceless. While they do not have to be life-changing, all the small impacts of new innovations will ultimately lead to a better place for us all. We all have an underlying desire to contribute to something greater than ourselves.

PART 3

EFFECT CHANGE

THE THIRD ATTRIBUTE IN THE FIT FOR DISRUPTION MODEL IS CHANGE.
This is your ability to adapt, transform and execute to deliver sustained
business performance. Ideas are only ideas until they're executed. Even
the best plans and ideas amount to nothing unless they are done. For
ideas to be done, you need people to engage with and embrace change,
not fight it. You need to be change-ready.

Being change-ready will enable your organisation to act with speed
and agility. Having change capability means that you can do more and
respond to market needs and challenges. Having a change culture will
ensure that you not only stay relevant, you also become a profitable
industry leader.

Unfortunately, however, most people don't like change; it makes us
uncomfortable. Many people will want to kick, scream, jump up and
down, and create so much distracting energy that change will be near
impossible. This resistance is driven mostly by fear.

The way to overcome fear of change is with understanding and engagement. Sometimes it is as simple as giving people the right tools or training
so that they can feel confident or helping them understand the importance of what it is that they are doing and how it fits the bigger picture.

If you can remove the fear of change from your organisation, and provide skills, support and momentum, you will be able to move mountains. The energy that is created by people pushing in one direction towards a common goal is priceless. When you have an organisation that embraces change like this, you can start lifting the bar and you can become bolder and braver in designing your business for future relevance and sustainability.

The key elements to being able to effect **CHANGE** in a disruptive, rapidly changing environment are:

1. **Lead the vision** and change effort – change must be led
2. **Build confidence** – people need to believe it can be done
3. **Empower the people** – set the people up for success
4. **Communicate effectively** – there can never be too much communication
5. **Build the right team** – build a team that can deliver

CHANGE MODEL

5. BUILD THE RIGHT TEAM – build a team that can deliver

1. LEAD the VISION and CHANGE EFFORT – change must be led

2. BUILD CONFIDENCE – people need to believe it can be done

3. EMPOWER PEOPLE – set people up for success

4. COMMUNICATE EFFECTIVELY – there can never be too much communication

CHAPTER 9

BE A LEADER

BEING CHANGE-READY IS A QUESTION OF CULTURE. AND CULTURE needs to be led. If it is not led it will fail and the organisation will find itself in a world of pain.

Leadership becomes the standard. When team members are trying to emulate behaviour, they will emulate that of their leaders. If leaders behave with integrity and respect, the team will do the same. If leaders behave poorly, then that sets the standard that it is okay for everyone else to behave poorly.

Leaders who have passion and direction and are values-led have the greatest opportunity to engage and inspire their people. People will connect with them, believe in them and, as a result, will move mountains for them.

A leader needs to demonstrate that the impossible is possible. Someone needs to push through the barrier of the burning, the aches and the hard times and demonstrate that it is well worth it. Often a leader will calm the team in moments of crisis, or madness. Leaders will influence and motivate everyone around a common goal. They will build respect and trust among all the team, both internal and external. A great leader will empathise and place people at the heart of everything that they do, because they know that without the collective effort of the team, change will not happen, whatever that change may be.

A leader will make the hard decisions, and the right ones. They will decide when to say no, when to slow down or speed up. They will speak up when something is not right and values do not align; they will sacrifice. They will ensure people are not used as a commodity; they will add value in every sense of the word.

HAVE A VISION

A clearly articulated vision will move people. A good leader will have a strong vision and clearly communicate it to their people.

While your vision does not have to be as emotional as, say, Martin Luther King's 'I have a dream' speech or as bold as John F Kennedy's 'We choose to go to the moon' speech, leadership will start with a vision. Show people where they are going and, importantly, why they are going there and how they are going to get there.

A change vision differs from your company vision, although themes will overlap, and they should be aligned. Both are extremely important. A company vision is enterprise-wide and focuses on the vision of the entire company. A change vision is primarily targeted at those who will be instrumental in delivering change, whereas the corporate vision may have broader appeal to a wider audience.

If it is embraced, a vision will permeate through all levels of the organisation. It will live in the actions, beliefs and values of the organisation and it will provide the framework for every action taken or not taken.

The vision becomes so much more than just a statement, a one-liner, or a moment in time. It becomes something that provides a purpose, a reason for being. People want to have a meaning and a purpose for doing what they do, particularly in their careers, which are such a big part of life. The vision becomes a call to action, the reason for getting out of bed, or the reason why you would push through discomfort rather than quit. Discomfort equals growth.

The vision helps the team to focus and understand where to place their energies and, just as importantly, where *not* to place their energies. It becomes a motivational force, something that is very difficult to quantify, but immeasurable in terms of its value.

The vision needs to be compelling. Something that moves people, gives them a reason to change their behaviour or to become curious about a different way of doing things. It needs to be able to help them focus their energy on key priorities. The vision will need to make sense and appeal to the stakeholders. The vision is not an exercise in meaningless statements, nor is it about trying to satisfy every stakeholder group – it is about finding a cause that resonates and directs people down a path. The vision will find common interests for all the stakeholder groups.

Industry leaders will understand what vision is required for the time, and timing can be very important. They will be able to 'read the room' and articulate a vision that is appropriate.

The vision will reflect *why* the change is so important. Often people are motivated to change because they are in crisis and there is no other option. For example, someone who receives a poor medical diagnosis may have no option but to change their diet or lifestyle habits. In a business context, change may be essential due to poor financial performance or competition from a new player in the marketplace. Many organisations have to make significant change because their industry or space is being disrupted. But it should not have to come to this, nor does it have to. Your organisation can and should be ahead of the curve. The very premise of this book, 'Fit for Disruption', is itself a burning platform; if organisations do not adapt, they will die.

But the reason for change can also be positive. A call to action does not have to be a 'burning platform' in the negative sense. Change can be motivated by a higher purpose or a greater opportunity. Perhaps a new market opportunity has opened, a new technology has become available, or an existing competitor has failed their customer base and now they are turning to you for support – which forces you to change by reorganising and scaling up.

Leaders need to be clear on the scope of change. You want people to be able to focus and to manage their efforts towards the goal. It is remarkably easy to get scope creep, and the best way to control this is to be clear from the outset on what it is you are trying to achieve. This is not to say that you have to be belligerent and fixed in your approach – there will always be moments that you need to pivot and adjust – but you do want to maintain the integrity of the program and ensure that the focus is moving towards the goal. Start with baby steps and quick wins to show that change is nothing to be afraid of.

A great change vision should include the following elements:

- The Why – articulate the reason for change;
- Outcomes – what is actually going to be achieved;
- What the outcomes will look like – what people are doing and how they are behaving in the new world;
- Feel – what people will feel in the future;
- Hope – the promise of a better future; and
- The Path – how you are going to get there.

Here is an example of a simple but strong change vision (as a hypothetical example):

'We aspire to be the number one sports apparel retailer in the world.

Our commitment is to deliver 10% Profit, 20% Growth and 25% return on capital.

Our business provides the greatest range of the best brands in sporting apparel for sports lovers.

Our growth will continue to come from online and international markets. We will always love bricks and mortar retailing and continue to offer that channel, but our growth and future lie in online retailing.

Our customers have told us that they love our brands and our pricing, but they want greater reliability and speed in the delivery of online product. They tell us that this is what will separate us from the rest.

From today until the start of 2023, we will invest $300 million in warehouse automation in four new purpose-built facilities across the nation.

This provides our company with the ability to service our customers faster than any of our competitors, despatching online orders within one hour of transaction. When we link this capability with our global delivery network, which is already considered best practice, we will be the fastest and most reliable online retailer, to any point in the globe, from this nation.

Not only will this delight our customers, the growth generated will provide massive opportunities for our people. We expect this growth to generate over 500 new jobs and allow us to invest $50 million in the best customer experience and leadership training the world has to offer.

We are also pleased to appoint Mary Smith to the role of Chief Transformation Officer. She will oversee, and be accountable for, this exciting initiative. Mary will assemble the best people and processes to make this organisational change effective.

We love technology, but we love people more. That is our difference.'

This relatively short vision can be extended to provide more context and detail. The trick here is to be very specific and very clear. The vision is painting a picture of what the future looks like; this helps people visualise not only the end state, but also what the transitions will look like.

RESPECT YOUR PEOPLE

A good leader respects the people they lead and understands how much their work affects their personal lives and sense of general wellbeing.

Work is a big part of our lives. Think about it. Often, when meeting someone for the first time, you're asked, 'What do you do?' When we meet family and friends, we ask, 'How is work going?' When we were children we were constantly asked, 'What do you want to be when you grow up?' It's odd how we always want to bring up the subject of work.

Work can have a profound effect on our personal lives – we don't all leave it behind come end of business hours. Many personal relationships fail because of the demands of work. Many parents miss their kids' sport or don't get to read them bedtime stories because of work commitments. Most of us rely on a regular pay cheque to buy necessities such as food and housing, but many people also identify themselves by their careers.

Work affects people's personal lives, so you should show that you understand this and create a flexible, tolerant workplace. You should also create a workplace where people want to be. You don't want them spending all day just waiting to go home, then dreading coming back the next day. It makes sense to create an environment that is supportive, that allows people some relief from the pressure that society places on them.

It makes for more cohesive teams, better-quality output, better problem solving and better solutions if people are happy at work. I am not talking running-around-in-daffodil-fields-type happy, but a general feeling of wellbeing and a positive mood.

Happy people are more effective; happy people create solutions, not problems; happy people are generally confident about sharing ideas – or speaking up if they see a train wreck coming. Happy people innovate. This is not to say that people won't have bad days – we all do – but if people are generally happy, they are more likely to be advocates for and engaged in change.

Even the World Economic Forum recognises that there is a strong correlation between employee wellbeing, productivity and organisational performance. In 2019, they published an article that quoted a number of scholarly research papers that support this idea. It was found that emotional states and sense of wellbeing affect productivity. More positive emotions enhance motivation and lead to better outcomes. Positivity leads to more creativity and wellbeing increases effort and productivity. [1]

It's also important that your employees feel safe – both physically and psychologically. When your care for your workers shows, they feel valued as human beings, not just employees, and are more likely to feel the respect for you that is essential for change leadership.

Feeling safe and secure is a fundamental human need. If your employees do not feel safe, it is most unlikely that there will be any contribution or engagement that can build value. It is also a fundamental element to the unwritten, unspoken contract in any

---

[1] World Economic Forum 2019, accessed 27 January, 2020, https://www.weforum.org/agenda/2019/07/happy-employees-and-their-impact-on-firm-performance/

relationship, whether personal or business. If safety is not valued, you or your organisation will not be valued because you are failing to provide a basic human need.

A poor safety culture will tell people, customers and other stakeholders that they are not worthy of respect. If they are not worthy of respect, why then should respect be offered in return? That is not how human behaviour works. Think of the reverse. If you have a very strong culture of safety, if you value people's wellbeing, it is most likely that the value will be reciprocated.

Psychological safety is also important. No one should feel bullied or blamed for something beyond their control. Allow people to respectfully speak their truth about what is on their mind. But remember that there is a difference between constructive feedback and negative, nasty or vindictive commentary. Negative talk can be a behavioural issue, which should be addressed, and the best way to do this is to encourage people to provide constructive and respectful feedback.

Transformative leaders require different thinking, and it makes no sense to shut down anyone's voice. If a leader shuts down the voice of one person, they will shut down the imagination of the entire organisation.

If your people do not feel safe, physically or psychologically, how can they possibly turn their attention to innovation? Their minds are obviously already preoccupied with trying to protect themselves.

REMOVE THE SHACKLES

As individuals, we carry around all sorts of limiting beliefs – all the 'why nots' and 'I cant's'. There is the 'I am too old', 'too young', 'not qualified enough', 'not experienced enough', 'others are already doing it', 'I have tried this before and failed', 'it's not the way the world works'.

Limiting beliefs are the enemy of change. But good leadership will help your people to overcome their limiting beliefs and believe that they can. It will instil a sense of inner belief that much is possible beyond what people tell themselves.

I am unsure what happens between childhood and adulthood, but for some reason we all create limiting beliefs. No doubt some of them are created to serve us, but many of them hold us back, and are often the root of much of our anxiety and frustration. Some people have more, or more acute, limiting beliefs than others. The more limiting beliefs are repeated, the more they are embedded, and the more we believe in them. It is a loop that produces the same outcome unless it can be short circuited.

And it can be. For example, I recently thought that because of my heavy travelling schedule, I did not have time to exercise or access to fresh, healthy food. This was my limiting belief and excuse for why I was becoming unhealthy. But it was nonsense. Once I reframed my beliefs, I realised that I only had to reorganise my diary to allow time for exercise. I could walk to a meeting instead of taking an Uber, or I could have a walking meeting in the park instead of the office. For food, all I had to do was ask the restaurant to steam my vegies and hold the fries.

Limiting beliefs don't just apply to individuals; they also apply to teams, functions and organisations. It may be the finance department that doesn't believe that they can provide creative solutions, or a team may think that they are not respected. One of the most common limiting beliefs about change is the 'we have tried that before and it doesn't work' belief. Another is: 'we don't have enough resources – time or money.' Regardless of who has a limiting belief or what the limiting belief is, it is your job as leader to help your people overcome these restrictions and encourage them to believe that they can change.

OFFER INCENTIVES

So far in this chapter I've been talking about leading your people by having a vision, by respecting them and by encouraging them to think big. But let's not forget the more down-to-earth methods of encouraging your people to come on board with your change initiatives. There is a place for a good old-fashioned carrot here, which is where incentives come in. But you need to be careful. Incentives are tricky things.

Many organisations, for whatever reason, develop functionally driven incentive schemes. It makes sense to align these with the objectives of the function, as a company-wide incentive is often simply too vague or too far removed from people's everyday work to resonate with them. There's a disconnect between their actions and decisions and the result that those actions and decisions produce.

There's also a danger that the incentive becomes more important than the broader goals of the company. Too often I have seen people make the wrong decision for the company because it would affect their incentive scheme. I have, time and time again, encountered product and sales professionals who will make decisions based on first level margin rather than net profit – that is, after the true cost to serve.

In the worst-case scenario, this behaviour can lead to fraudulent and criminal activity. The honey is just too inviting for some. Money and greed will make people do things that they would never have thought were in their capability to do.

Used the right way, however, an incentive scheme can be useful. I once had a very successful year personally, and the company had a bumper year. My incentive scheme was uncapped, and the way the numbers fell meant I literally earned my salary again in an incentive. What was interesting about this, however, is that it didn't change my behaviour or decision making one bit for the year that incentive period applied. While I did not expect the incentive, nor did I feel an entitlement to it, receiving it did give me a very strong sense of inclusion and respect. I felt that I was truly part of the success of the organisation. I became vested into the future.

If you have an incentive scheme, don't set targets that are unattainable, or which will be met regardless of the individual or team's performance, contribution or behaviour. Keep it very simple, very transparent and very fair. You can offer incentives in different forms – such as allocating time to a charity, or staff lunches and the like.

Whatever the incentive structure in your organisation, it needs to align with the outcome you want for the entire organisation, and one metric in one function should not contradict another metric in another function. Ensure that the incentives are aligned with the company strategy and performance, and that they promote positive action in areas such as safety, governance, cultural behaviours and, of course, the high standard of the organisation's values (and that of modern society).

> ## The first step in becoming a Change-ready organisation is to lead the vision and change effort.

You must start with a strong vision that outlines the reasons why the change needs to happen, and how the organisation will move towards that vision. The vision will be clear and will appeal to the emotional sentiments of the audience. The vision will be so simple that everybody will be able to understand it and know how they can contribute to achieving it. It needs to be a vision that people can buy into and want to see happen.

WHAT YOU CAN DO

- ☑ As with your strategy and strategic plan, you need to have a clearly articulated vision for your key initiative program. The vision and action plan need to link back to the overarching strategy and strategic plan. In other words, this change strategy and plan will be a subset of the organisation's overarching plan – but at an initiative level;

- ☑ Lead from the front – demonstrate the actions and behaviours expected;

- ☑ Get very interested in the safety and wellbeing of your team;

- ☑ Develop big thinking capability – and identify limiting beliefs in individuals and teams; and

- ☑ Align incentive programs with the strategic objectives of the organisation.

CHAPTER 10

BUILD CONFIDENCE

OFTEN, WHEN UNDERGOING A TRANSFORMATION, FACING HIGH levels of uncertainty or embarking on a highly ambitious plan, people want to feel that it can be achieved and that their efforts will not be in vain. A great leader will instil confidence in the people they are leading.

There are many ways to generate this confidence, and many ways that it can be undermined. For a start, you should be able to demonstrate a sound plan and an understanding of how the vision can be achieved. Being able to attract good people, access resources or even get some early traction on the plan all help build the confidence narrative.

A leader needs to do something to demonstrate that they mean business. Often people are disengaged because they have heard it all before, and don't believe that you'll walk the talk. Being able to show that this time it's different, through a symbolic action that demonstrates a shift and commitment to the vision, can resonate with people who are looking for that confidence. A symbolic action could be the hiring of the required talent, investments in specific resources or perhaps closing an underperforming site.

People can smell insecurity and lack of confidence. They will be looking for all the subtle cues, such as body language and tone of voice, that might give you away. If the leaders themselves don't really believe in the vision, then that will ultimately be its undoing – even if it had genuine merit. But don't let this alarm you or make you think that you must not put a foot wrong. People are not looking for perfection in leadership – they are looking for authenticity, commitment and, ultimately, confidence. They want honest communication – whether the news is good or bad.

CREATE TRUST

A symbolic action by a leader is a good way to signal that they mean business with their change initiative, but they must also take the time to build trust.

Humans are designed to trust in order to survive. In a tribal setting, when humans were vulnerable to wild animals, some members of the tribe slept while others kept watch. If you did not trust your tribe and you felt that you needed to sleep with one eye open, you would not have a very harmonious or happy life. Those tribal instincts are alive in us today, and although we no longer need protection from sabre-toothed tigers, we want to feel protected from outside threats that may hurt us. We want to feel safe, and to feel safe we need to be able to trust.

In the context of business, the company is the tribe, the competitors are external threats, and it is the leader who keeps watch and instils trust. A disruptive, rapidly changing environment can feel acutely threatening. So, trust becomes essential for a change initiative to be successful. Teams need to have trust in their leaders and in each other. They need to trust that they are going in the right direction for the right reasons. They also need to know that they will be protected and that they will be helped to prosper.

Trust takes time to build, and you need to be careful not to destroy it. If people are constantly taken on a journey that hits dead ends, or where leaders abandon ship at the slightest hint of complexity or hardship, trust will be lost. If employees are used as sacrificial lambs to protect the people in power within the organisation, trust will be destroyed in a stroke. Throwing someone under the bus undermines the trust in everyone, not just the people involved. The fear becomes contagious.

What happens when you don't have trust is that people will become very selfish and start taking decisions and matters into their own hands. They will make decisions that will ensure their own survival within the organisation, or within whatever frame is appropriate. Bad leaders will then blame them and fail to look within, and so the vicious cycle is perpetuated

But when you have trust, people are prepared to forego, they are prepared to add extra effort, they will tell you the truth and they will act in the interests of the goals. The goals can't be some corporate wish-washy statement that is all about profit, however. Your people will want to attach their trust to something that has real purpose, which is why your Why and your vision are important.

BUILD MOMENTUM

Momentum builds. How many dominoes do you think it would take to knock over the Empire State Building? A million? A billion? An experiment was set up with a series of thirteen dominoes, the first of which was five millimetres tall and one millimetre thick. Each subsequent domino was roughly 1.5 times the size of the preceding domino. The gravitational pull from knocking over the first small domino would continue to build as each domino fell. If this sequence was continued, the twenty-ninth domino would be the size of the Empire State Building.

Just as momentum builds, success compounds. Success works the same way as the falling dominoes – lots of small and frequent wins will compound and help success grow at an exponential rate.

Getting a win, and consistent wins, does much for the psychology of your people and of your organisation. It provides credibility and proof that you are not just talking the talk, but that there is real movement. We all attach ourselves to the tangible, and we have great difficulty with the intangible. Nothing will focus people more than a win that is an indisputable fact – the event has occurred. And people want to be associated with success. The more successful you are, the more your people will trust your leadership and feel confident about your change initiative.

For each success there will be learnings – what worked, what didn't, what improvements can be made, who else could have contributed. It allows the process of iteration to build upon itself. The small wins, by compounding, then become medium-sized wins with each iteration and development, which will then morph into a much larger win purely because the product, service or process has had bugs and deficiencies ironed out.

Once you have people on board and are getting some wins, you will be surprised at how quickly the momentum shifts. Better still is that you will start tapping into people's hidden potential, which will start emerging because they feel safer and more confident.

The market will start getting wind that change is underway, and that has positive results. You will find that you start attracting better talent, better customers and better suppliers. It will also lead to better commercial outcomes as you have better quality, more-engaged people, which, in turn, will lead to better innovation capability and more things changing for the good. It is all circular.

As you continue to work through your change initiative, however, you must be careful that quick wins don't become band aids. There is a risk that these efforts will become tokenistic and will be pursued just to tick a box that says the organisation is focused on innovation. There are many organisations that are ploughing significant money and resources into creating innovation capability, expecting that this is something that you can buy. Investment is absolutely required in terms of financial resource and time, but unless there is real leadership support, starting from the highest level and permeating through the organisation, it becomes a futile exercise.

If your leadership team shows fragility at the first sign of failure, or impatience with results that are not immediate, embedding an innovation culture will be hard to achieve. The objective is to create a culture that can embrace innovation and be able to change and innovate fast, but the capability needs to be built gradually and on firm foundations. Without these foundations, progress will be short-lived.

You must also select the right innovation. If you just select a random process or product to innovate that does not connect with your overall vision for the company, the exercise becomes not only pointless, but also damaging as it wastes resources and annoys a lot of the people who are trying to add value to your organisation. If you alienate these people, it will take you much longer to get them back on side when you are ready to focus on innovation properly. You may even lose them altogether, as they will form a view and question what they signed up for.

You also need to deal with failure correctly. Unless you have a structure in place to learn from your failures, your failures will compound just like your successes. This will cause people to lose confidence and resources will be constrained. The best antidote to compounding failure is to learn, and to learn quickly and consistently.

Creating an innovation movement takes some time and cannot simply be a click of the fingers. Nor is it something that can be bought. Developing a culture takes immense patience and resilience and requires an inner belief that it is the right thing to do.

SUSTAIN THE CHANGE

As the momentum of your change initiative builds, so will confidence. But once the momentum is built, you need to ensure that you can sustain the change. This is also important in building confidence. You need to have a system and culture to sustain it. It is unlikely that people will change behaviours or engage in a change process if they think that the change won't stick. Don't make the mistake of thinking that once the implementation is done, that's it.

Reasons why a change might not be sustained include:

- Not having buy-in and engagement;
- Being unrealistic in the first place;
- Cutting funding after the implementation;
- Leaders' attention and support going elsewhere, which sends a subtle message that the change is no longer important;
- The change being single-point sensitive. It relies on a particular leader, operator or team and cannot be sustained after they leave; and
- The process not being documented, embedded and continuously improved – it becomes outdated the day it has been implemented.

If the organisation has a habit of implementing change programs, whether cultural or process based, only to revert back to the status quo, employees start to lose confidence in future programs. How many times have you heard 'We tried that before and it didn't last'? And if people in the organisation cannot see that the change will last, they are unlikely to invest their time, energy, efforts and emotions into the change.

However, there are some very simple and practical ways that change can be sustained over the long term. Some of these include:

- Having leaders who support the change and maintain communication well after implementation;
- Having leaders who see that the change is actually taking place – they go to a site and observe the change in action;
- Addressing problems associated with the change – only a small adjustment may be required;

- Ensuring the change is repeatable and embedding it systemically into your culture and/or work practices;
- Introducing metrics and visual performance tools that make the ongoing performance visible and measurable;
- Introducing change sustainability to individual/team accountabilities and performance measures;
- Communicating and celebrating the wins – share the achievement;
- Realising the benefits – if people can see that benefits are realised, and the initiative is not just change for change's sake, they are more likely to stay with it;
- Implementing a continuous improvement program so that focus remains on the initiative or cultural change; and
- Embedding the change as part of your ongoing induction and training programs.

The second step in building a Change-ready organisation is to build confidence.

To mobilise change, you need to give people the confidence that it can be done. This does not mean that an ambitious vision needs to be watered down – it means that you give people concrete proof that it can be done and will be done. This can be achieved by having a very solid plan and great people leading it and demonstrating real movement towards the vision through quick wins and other actions that create momentum and value. It needs to be physical and real as early as possible and include everyone so that they can quickly start to believe in what will be delivered. Help people understand that they are safe, and that their needs will be met.

WHAT YOU CAN DO

☑ Begin the change with a symbolic action and immediately start working on quick wins;

☑ Identify and start removing obstacles;

☑ Plan how you will take people on the journey of change, considering individual and team needs;

☑ Build complete transparency into your communications; and

☑ Establish a framework that instils confidence that the change will be sustained.

CHAPTER 11

EMPOWER YOUR PEOPLE

YOU CAN HAVE THE MOST SOUND COMMERCIAL BASE FOR YOUR business and the most exciting, innovative ideas you could possibly imagine, but those ideas will just be ideas if you don't make them happen. A very important change leadership competency is the ability to empower people to get the job done. However, it is obviously quite dangerous to just leave your teams to the task if they do not have all the tools and support they need. You must be able to set your teams up for success. You want leaders and managers in your organisation to be able to lead change in their respective areas. They cannot do this if they do not have the necessary skills in change leadership or in change management. You need to make sure that your leaders have all the competencies that they require and, if they do not have them, that they know where and how to get them. They also need to be familiar with all the tools and techniques in change management so that they can confidently execute on the change plan.

To empower your teams, you also need to give them appropriate resources, and enough resources. Creativity and innovation cannot solve every single problem; your people need money and resources to get the job done in the designated timeframe. While you do not want to be wasteful, you do want to ensure that you give your teams a fighting chance of success. If you fail to give access to appropriate resources, you also run the risk of alienating and disengaging the very people that you need to be motivated and passionate about the change.

SHOW YOUR SUPPORT

Support can come in many forms, from what is said and communicated through to making resources available or removing obstacles. A resource may be funding, it may be people, it may even be time.

Resource includes leadership support. Getting significant change through can often be a long, lonely road with many obstacles and difficulties. Dealing with change-resistant people can be exhausting and dealing with snipers and passive aggressive behaviour can take a toll. Leadership support empowers people. That support can help your leaders through low periods and carry them to the next gate. While it is important that your change leaders have the resilience and skills to cope with the ups, downs, disappointments and even elations of a change program, you must not use this as an excuse to withdraw visible support.

If people in the organisation suspect the executive leadership are wavering in their support, it will place the entire change initiative in jeopardy. It may be that executives are incentivised on short-term financial performance or are too focused on quick and easy wins that look good today without thinking of the future. They may be under significant pressure from the board or other parties. But unless everyone in the organisation is demonstrating an unwavering commitment to the initiative, you may as well not bother. There is nothing more disempowering than having leadership desert in times of need, and it is often at these critical junctures that the success of a change initiative is made or broken. Showing support demonstrates that the leadership is committed to the change, and that the people delivering the change are valued and important. You also need to be careful that your support does not take the form of whip-cracking.

While having a sense of urgency can be a great thing, placing undue stress and anxiety onto a situation will only lead to compromised input and outcomes, running the risk of burning people out or completely disengaging them. Pressure does not mean effectiveness. Standing there barking orders and telling people to hurry up will most likely paralyse any positive behaviour and action.

Make sure that your organisation or the teams that are affected by the change are ready for the change. You can't have them at full capacity and focused on business-as-usual activity and then overlay an important change initiative without giving them the space to be able to work on it.

Maybe the program is hitting a very busy patch, in which case the path should be cleared of distractions, noise or interference. You may have to quiet the noise, remove the distractions, silence the unfair critics and build the energy.

Helping your change leaders to set priorities is another form of support. There needs to be laser-like focus, because many things half done is not success. Support is shown by ensuring that the business is aligned with the priorities. It is not very supportive to send out your team to deliver and have the rest of your organisation swimming in the other direction. Helping to expedite decisions shows support.

Communication provides support. You must communicate your support to your change leaders not just once at the beginning of the change effort, but regularly and consistently for its duration. You need to show unwavering support throughout all the challenges. Leaders must walk the talk and behave in a way consistent with the messages being delivered. Your teams need to understand the change and how it is going to occur, what is expected of them and how the change will impact them, their team or their colleagues. They may have many questions that need answering.

Your presence is a type of communication, and leaders should also show outward, physical signs of support when the need arises. It will be about being there at key team talks, showcases and go-lives. Remaining calm and poised in tough times is an important form of support. No change program will go exactly to plan. Often there will be bumps and bends in the road, and having an expectation that it is a straight line to success is both naïve and unhelpful. Your calm demeanour in times of trouble will help the confidence of the teams delivering the change and can help silence the critics.

Dealing with problematic team members shows support. There may be some dissidents or game-players in the ranks, who should be managed or removed. There will be the bullies, there will be the passive aggressive types, and there will be the people who will jump on every opportunity to discredit, negatively disrupt or simply white-ant an initiative. Or they may attack the credibility of the program or the people tasked with executing the change. While you want to encourage strong debate and engagement and ensure that risks and issues are called out in a trusted and safe environment, there is no place for people who actively try to bring the change effort down to satisfy their own ego or private agenda. You need to show that this behaviour will not be tolerated.

When an initiative or program of work is delivered, things may be missed, and mistakes will be made. A supportive manager does not judge when mistakes are made, but instead helps everyone learn from the experience. No one is perfect and, provided the greater cause of the change is worth fighting for, resilience and unwavering support need to be shown.

The support you show must be truthful. Be extremely honest about the change, and why it is occurring and the potential impacts. If you're honest about potential bad news, people will be more willing to sacrifice self-interest for the greater good. Dishonesty diminishes all levels of support.

TRAIN YOUR PEOPLE

Anything that requires a level of mastery or competence requires training, and ongoing training. This applies equally to sports, music, aviation or vocations such as medicine, engineering or law. Training is key. Training provides the new skills that will be required in a changing workplace. Without fail, the change programs I have been in that invested heavily in training and development have been 100 per cent successful. The programs I have been involved in that have compromised on training and development have been unmitigated disasters.

Yet, when there are major programs in place and major changes to the way people and teams conduct their roles and how they integrate with an organisation, more often than not, those who are required to change are handed a document and a few encouraging words to excite them into changing. They have no idea why, how or what to change. They do not understand how the change will impact them at an operational level, despite needing to understand the risks and situations they may find themselves in with customers and other stakeholders. Untrained team members have low production value, are inefficient and may be unable to execute the task or help customers.

People who are directly affected by a change must be trained in the new method or new equipment. No matter how easy you think a change can be, at an operational level there are many permutations and variables at play that make it critical to help the user with the transition. Hopefully, they have already been engaged at a testing level but, when it comes to actual roll-out of the initiative, it is important to help them through the change step by step.

Training comes in many forms, and, while classroom training has its place, most of it should be on-the-job, real-life training. Seventy per cent of knowledge will be obtained from job-related experience, twenty per cent from interactions with others and ten per cent from formal educational activities. Remember that people will have different learning styles. For instance, some people learn by listening and absorbing, others may be visual learners – you may need to show them a diagram, a picture or even demonstrate how something is done – and others, of course, learn by doing. Some people will ask lots of questions, others won't, some will take no time at all to grasp new concepts and tasks, and others may need quite a lot of time.

It is also important to remember that people start with different levels of knowledge, so you will need to calibrate and align your training accordingly. You don't want to tell people how to suck eggs, and you also don't want to deliver training to an audience that has no idea what you are talking about.

Frontline people in particular may receive complaints about the change from customers and service providers, so they should be trained and equipped to deal with the situation. When plastic bags were being phased out by supermarkets in Australia, the poor check-out staff were abused by shoppers who forgot to bring their own bags. The supermarket team members needed to be prepared for that reaction from the customers and trained appropriately to manage the situation.

Allow people time to come to grips with what is being asked of them. Have advocates and respected peers teaching. Give people the chance to learn, to master their craft and, if not, at least ensure that they can perform their work to a level that does not diminish their self-esteem or affect customers or service providers.

Ultimately, you want the user not only to embrace the change, but also to sustain the change. If you do not invest in training, the user is likely to revert to old practices or find workarounds that defeat the purpose of the change. You want them to be asking for more change, not trying to avoid it. And training should never finish – it should be systemic in your organisation and simply performing a task should be considered a learning opportunity.

One final point on the topic of training your people – this is an ongoing commitment, and not something that is done once and then forgotten. Innovative organisations have a commitment to learning and developing – all the time.

GET OUT OF THE WAY

'It doesn't make sense to hire smart people and then tell them what to do; we hire smart people so they can tell us what to do.'
STEVE JOBS

Your main role as a leader is to create the environment, the connections and the culture for the organisation to prosper. Then you should get out of the way and let people get on with it. If people need to be watched over every minute of the day, there will be something wrong with the leadership style and approach.

Having the humility to step aside and allow others to flourish is not an easy thing for many leaders to do, particularly when things look wobbly. There will always be a time and a place for you to be intensely involved, but unless you can build an organisation, product or process that can survive and prosper without you, you have not created a legacy.

From a purely financial perspective, a lot of money goes into hiring clever people who can help you achieve your organisational goals. If you alone, or with your leadership group, are going to disempower them by making all the decisions and professing to be the authority on all things, the question must be asked why you are investing in these capable resources. Are you even hiring properly in the first place?

If you are the expert, it may be particularly hard to step away. But if you don't, it will become impossible to scale your initiative. It would be completely exhausting having to be involved in every tiny detail and to make, or be involved in, all the decisions as you expand. It would be impossible to scale to any meaningful level if the business, product or process is single-point sensitive.

It again gets down to designing your organisation so that it is not reliant on any one person or group. It is about designing empowerment into your business and culture. There will need to be some checks and balances, but the primary objective should always be to get the vision, strategy and buy-in right up front. Then, assuming you have people on board, they will self-manage and self-regulate.

Measure and monitor the things that matter most; don't measure and monitor your lack of trust – if you do, you may as well give up now because distrust is not a sustainable business model.

REMOVE THE HIERARCHIES

It's not just you as leader who has to get out the way. You also need to have the right management structure. Flattening hierarchies can help your organisation to respond rapidly to the economic climate. Too many layers of management and decision points, while well-intended, actually restrict an organisation's ability to be agile and make rapid improvements. Even without the decision points, the more layers there are, the greater the communication complexity, not to mention the costs associated with maintaining surplus layers of management.

Another reason for implementing a flat structure is to further empower team members to implement their ideas and ways of working, and be accountable for that, provided they deliver the desired results and do not impede the vision or culture of the organisation.

Empowerment is also about allowing your team to make the right choices for the betterment of the company without having to go through bureaucracy and red tape. American Airlines cabin crew can give out airline miles on the spot to address a customer service issue, such as an entertainment system not working. At Zappos, every employee is empowered to make good on an issue with a customer however that employee sees fit (without the need for ridiculous policy documents). Team members of the Ritz-Carlton can address problems immediately by providing upgrades, free stays and gifts up to the value of $2,000.

Empowerment implies trust, and when people feel trusted, they will assume a greater level of responsibility and engagement.

The third step in building a Change-ready organisation is to empower people.

The organisation needs to be empowered to deliver the change. There is a time to set the vision and to lead the way, however, you also need to know when to step back and let those best-equipped get on with it. They need the right resources, tools and time to make it happen. They will need support, guidance and structure so that they can keep on track. When the organisation is empowered to deliver the change, the change will be sustained because it will be owned by the people who are delivering it.

WHAT YOU CAN DO

- ☑ Outwardly demonstrate commitment and support for your team and change effort;
- ☑ Sit down with your team to determine what support they need;
- ☑ Establish a formal training program for all levels of the organisation that are affected by the change;
- ☑ Literally take a step back and allow your people to do what they need to do – ensure that they have the necessary support, tools and resources available; and
- ☑ Remove hierarchies and cut the red tape that may hold back your change initiative.

CHAPTER 12

COMMUNICATE, COMMUNICATE, COMMUNICATE

YOUR PEOPLE ARE NOT MUSHROOMS, SO DON'T KEEP THEM IN THE dark and feed them sh*t. You need to be open and honest about the change initiative that's being rolled out. You need to communicate with all the people affected by it – openly, honestly and regularly. And you need to ensure that your communication is conducted in the right format, with the right tone and at the right time.

The key to communication is that a message is not communicated until it is understood. Regardless of the method of communication, you will need to go to great lengths to ensure that the message has been communicated in the manner in which it was intended. If not, there need to be some questions asked about either the method of communication or the message itself. We have two ears and one mouth for very good reasons, and we should perhaps use them in that proportion – remembering that communication is not one-way.

In today's world of hyper-information, you need your message to stand out, and you will need to be very creative in the way you distribute your communication so that you gain the attention of your audience.

COMMUNICATE CLEARLY AND CONSISTENTLY

The best change leadership comes with strong, consistent communication.

The communication style needs to be able to permeate all levels of the organisation, both internal and external. It is amazing how many leaders still try to complicate their communications, perhaps because they feel the need to over-intellectualise the message to justify their own position. The best communications are the ones that are simple and can be understood throughout the organisation.

There needs to be consistency across your messages, and they need to be put in a form that people can understand – in other words, without all the jargon and rhetoric. The simpler the communication, the easier it is for people to understand and to grasp what is required of them. You may have people in different sites, even in different countries, who need to understand and comprehend the communication and what it means.

Communication needs to be regular and consistent in timing. You want to be able to provide updates at every opportunity so that everyone understands the status and progress of the change initiative, and how it will affect them.

Different types of communication suit different circumstances. Sometimes it will be face-to-face communication; at other times, it may be group sessions, and you may want to issue company newsletters and updates.

The more involved someone is in the change effort, the more you will need to communicate with them. Depending on their involvement or the effect that the initiative will have on them, different audiences will require different types of communication.

There will be times that communications need to be upbeat, positive and motivational. At other times, communications may simply involve listing and working through all the actions and activities required for a new procedure. Or you might have to deliver some bad news, in which case a high degree of discretion, respect and consideration needs to be shown.

Change programs can be high-pressure environments where things do not always go to plan, or where issues arise that cause concern for stakeholders. People may express themselves badly when under pressure; they can alienate the people who are there to help them achieve their goals. Don't let yourself fall into this trap.

If people are kept in the dark or are constantly surprised, they will lose confidence and engagement in the process. Often people don't mind hearing bad news; they just need the information in a format that they can consume and that helps them understand what it means for them and what they are required to do, if anything.

You should also avoid falling into the trap of assuming that, once you have communicated something, people have understood. Checks need to be put in place to ensure that the message is being received as intended. There are many ways of doing this, such as asking for direct feedback or observing an environment to ascertain whether your people's actions and behaviours reflect what has been communicated.

Communications is a crucial area, but also something that many people have difficulty with. Here's a quick rundown of some of the more important factors in good communications:

- Be clear and concise in your communications;
- Remove noise and information clutter – don't talk about what is not important;
- Be specific about what you want people to do, and when;
- Don't wait to communicate important developments;
- Tell the truth – while you don't want to alarm people, you also need to be honest and authentic. Communicate the impacts from a change initiative, both good and bad, as soon as practicable;
- Avoid hearsay – communications must be direct;
- Get people in the same room, or on the same call, if there is a disagreement;
- Have consistent, company-wide communications that update the entire business on progress – including wins, achieving key milestones or general updates;
- Develop an information portal where stakeholders can self-serve information;
- Have leadership go on a 'Change Roadshow' that allows them to get face to face with the organisation and communicate in person. If this is not possible, video delivery may be required with an in-person presentation from a local leader;
- Develop a consistent rhythm of steering committees, key forums, meetings and team huddles;
- Don't have meetings for meetings' sake; respect people's time;
- Don't bombard people's inboxes with unnecessary emails. People tend not to pay attention to them. Instead, have a conversation – go see them or pick up the phone;
- The more important the communication, the more important

it is that you communicate in person;

- Dress appropriately when communicating in person – don't wear a suit and tie on the manufacturing floor, and don't wear your Friday casuals in the boardroom; and
- Have some fun and develop a 'brand' for your project initiative – logo, email signatures, t-shirts, stationery.

TALK TO YOUR STAKEHOLDERS

You will need to consider the impacts that the change initiative will have on your stakeholders, and how you can help them along the change journey. One thing is for sure, you will underestimate the number of stakeholders that will be affected, and you will most certainly underestimate the influence some of your stakeholders will have. Without a doubt, there will be a stakeholder whose importance to the initiative you have grossly underestimated. Imagine developing a brilliant product with an outstanding marketing plan supporting it, but failing to communicate with your logistics department, only to find that they do not have the capacity to deliver your new innovative product. It is a cardinal sin not to involve the actual operators or users, and while this example may seem silly, it does happen.

The more stakeholders you can bring on board early in the change process, the greater the groundswell and momentum will be. Onboarded and engaged stakeholders will do the heavy lifting for you through the change program.

There is a balance here, however, and many people misunderstand the stakeholder engagement process. It is often approached on an 'us versus them' basis, with a belief that the stakeholder must be convinced of or manipulated into a particular way of thinking – rather than have them come on board and support the initiative simply because it is, in fact, a good idea. This approach quickly becomes exhausting, and it is also impractical and does nothing to build sustainability in what you are trying to achieve.

The other mistake people make is trying to please every stakeholder and satisfy every single one of their unreasonable demands. This is impractical and unrealistic. You will not be able to make everyone happy, and while you should try, you are unlikely to succeed 100 per cent. However, effective change can still happen with unhappy stakeholders. The key here is communicating with them the right way and helping them to understand the impacts of the change initiative. They may not like it, but if they can sense that the change is for the greater good, they will deal with it. They just need to understand why it's happening, and what the steps are to get there.

A practical way to identify how to communicate with different stakeholder groups is to do some stakeholder analysis and mapping. It does not have to be complicated at all, just a simple quadrant that helps map stakeholders or stakeholder groups.

On the X axis you will have the INFLUENCE of the stakeholder, and on the Y axis you will have the INTEREST LEVEL of the stakeholder. All the stakeholders or stakeholder groups can then be plotted, which will help you manage them. Once plotted, the stakeholder or stakeholder groups will fall into one of the four categories:

1. Keep fully informed
2. Manage closely and work together
3. Anticipate and meet needs
4. Regular but minimal contact

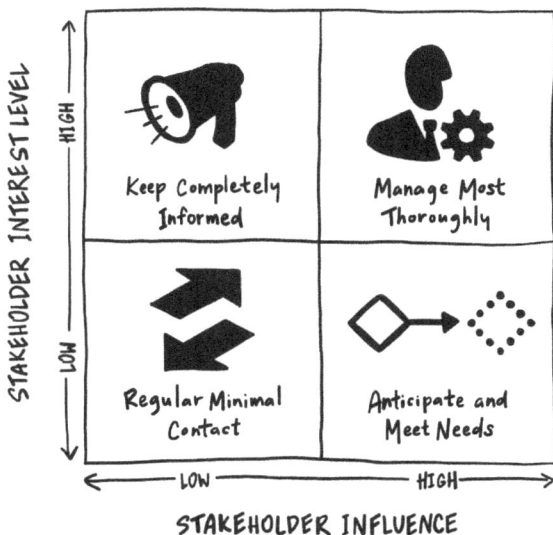

Mapping your stakeholders is only part of the process, however. You also should have a communication plan for each stakeholder group.

Keep your communications very simple. Identify the stakeholder, or group of stakeholders, and make sure you understand the impact that the change will have on them and the influence that they have. Then, determine the best way to engage with them and get their buy-in. If it is unlikely that you can get their buy-in, think about how you can manage the risks of them disrupting the change effort and what level of engagement and support that they will need.

PERSUADE THE DOUBTERS

With any large-scale change, you will certainly encounter your fair share of resistors. But don't ignore them – if you want to convert them to the cause, you need to communicate with them. In these cases, your communication should take the form of persuasion.

People can always find reasons why something is not perfect, however, I would try to draw their attention to whether the status quo is a better alternative. Instead of making your communications all about the new initiative, focus on what is wrong with the status quo and why it needs to change. Often people are waiting for the perfect solution, however, the perfect solution does not exist, so communicate what is currently being improved and how it is being improved. I have often found that negativity around a new initiative was easily overcome with one question: Is the business better off with or without this initiative?

Sometimes the impact of change may, in fact, be negative to a stakeholder group. In this case, you will need to give them the bigger picture and help them understand that the whole is greater than the sum of the parts. Most people are willing to bear the brunt of the personal impact to them if they can be sure it is for the greater good – but they need to understand what that is. If they don't buy into the greater good for selfish reasons, it becomes a cultural fit issue as opposed to a change issue.

For one reason or another, there will always be some people you cannot convert no matter how much you try and how compelling the case for change is. Provided there is no legitimate reason for the negativity (and you will need to critically evaluate your own bias), there will be times that you need to just move on and let these people make their own choices about their future. In extreme cases, you may need to decide their future for them, depending upon how important the change is or how disruptive these people are. The test is to make sure that your decision is in line with your values and behaviours, and with the cultural expectation in the context of what you are trying to achieve.

You should continue to give people an opportunity to get on board at every step in the process, but if you have to make the difficult decision to let someone go, it is important that you communicate why the decision has been made. If you don't communicate why, your strength and resilience may be interpreted as arrogance. But when people realise that the leader's resilience will not fail, they often develop a deeper level of respect.

SHOW, DON'T TELL

Communication can be more than verbal. It doesn't always have to be an email, a newsletter or a phone call. *Showing* people the change – what to expect from it, what will be different, how it will affect them – is critically important if you want to get their engagement and buy-in.

Many change initiatives fail because they don't show the key stakeholders all the benefits. You can do all the talking you like, but unless people can touch and feel the change, it will be hard for them to comprehend what is going to happen. Everyone has an imagination, and people can interpret the same set of facts differently. Understanding can be influenced by someone's mood, by their opinion of the person communicating the message, the content of what is being communicated or even the length and method of the communication. But showing people the change will help to keep your message consistent and accurate.

It is also a natural reflex of most adults to get frustrated at being told what to do. It can make us feel as if we don't have worthwhile opinions or that we're not respected. Showing someone the change, rather than just telling them to get on with it, makes people more likely to accept it, especially if they have an opportunity to provide an opinion. Even if their opinion is not taken on board, they will feel listened to. But this can't be done in a one-way *communication* – it needs to be a two-way *experience*.

You need to create an environment where people can engage in discussion, help articulate the problem and participate in developing the solution. They should be able to touch and feel prototypes, samples or even attend a centre of learning or excellence where the change has been implemented and can demonstrate what it means for the rest of the group.

Many people learn experientially. It will help these people accept and get on board with a change initiative if they can touch and feel the change, see how it will operate, and offer suggestions and feedback. When this happens, everyone feels like they are part of the initiative and they have a sense of ownership over what is happening.

It is a fine balance, though; it can take people a long time to engage with something new, and sometimes it is a near impossible task to show every single person what the change looks like. Where the change only affects a few people, you may be able to show them the change in person. But if the change affects thousands of people, you may have to put your creative mind to how you will best communicate effectively. It all depends on how big the change is, and how many people will be affected.

The fourth step in creating a Change-ready organisation is to communicate effectively.

The key to effective change is to communicate. There is no such thing as over-communication. The communication starts at concept stage and does not stop – it needs to be relentless. The messages need to be understood, not just heard. The communications need to stand out from all the noise and need to attract the attention of the audience.

WHAT YOU CAN DO

- ☑ Build an extensive communication and stakeholder management plan;
- ☑ Identify resistance points, and act on them quickly;
- ☑ Have leadership walk and show the vision in an operational setting or environment where the problem or solution may exist; and
- ☑ Give people the opportunity to 'get off the bus', and for those that are on it – insist on their commitment.

CHAPTER 13

BUILD THE RIGHT
CHANGE TEAM

HUMAN CAPITAL IS THE BIGGEST INVESTMENT THAT AN ORGANISA-
tion can make. It is all about the right people with the right mindset
in the right roles doing the right things at the right time with the
right tools.

Serious thought needs to be given to how to mobilise transformation
leaders and teams, the roles they play and the responsibilities and
accountabilities they will have in the process. You want advocates,
leaders, people with positive vibe and energy. You also want people
with some expertise and knowledge, those with hope and those who
see things differently. Most of all, you need people who will make
it happen and help those who don't want to make it happen to get
out of the way. Building an effective change team is critical if you
want to have a change-ready organisation.

Change cannot be outsourced; it must be done by your organisation's people, not by outsiders. You can provide the operators with
outside support, but you cannot have outside support deliver the
change. If you want to get change done, you need to make sure

your organisation, the teams and the individuals are ready for the change and have the capacity to embrace and deliver continuous change, sustainably.

YOUR CHANGE TEAM

Heading your change team will be **official leadership sponsors**. These are the leaders who are accountable at an executive level for making the change happen. A sponsor must be a member of the organisation's leadership team. If a member of the leadership team cannot be appointed as a project sponsor, then the question must be asked about priorities and focus.

Sometimes sponsors are given their sponsor position despite having no vested interest in the success or failure of the change. They must be capable of sponsoring, have influencing and mentoring skills, and be able to coach and lead the project teams. They need to be actively engaged, not tokenistic; they need to be driving and passionately pushing the change along.

These leadership sponsors will help remove the barriers to change and provide support in times of need. They will also provide structured guidance and be visible. You need to choose the right people.

You should also have **unanointed leaders and change champions**. These are people who are respected and influential in the organisation, and whose opinions and thoughts are highly regarded. If these people are on board, others will follow because they trust them. It does not matter where these leaders sit in the hierarchy, as long as people trust them and listen to them. If these leaders are advocating for the success of the change, you are halfway down the journey. They will not block unless there is good reason to do so, and if they see there is a benefit they will fight for that benefit so that all can enjoy the fruits of the effort. They also can influence and pull into line people who are negatively disrupting. These leaders and change champions will likely come from the operational areas of the business, but may also sit in support functions, or perhaps be leaders themselves. Generally, they volunteer, or need little persuasion to join the movement. They may even assume the role without any formal appointment – they just become advocates through their own volition.

Project teams need to be made up of people who have the relevant expertise, perspectives and influence to make the change happen. Generally, these will need to have cross-functional representations. These teams not only require technical expertise, but must also be able to spur their colleagues into action within the functional teams. The project team needs to be empowered to make the change happen.

You also need **diversity** in the team and you may need **external contribution**; you may need to bring outsiders in for a different perspective. This needs to be managed carefully, however, as it can be viewed as a threat and, consequently, disrupt the change process itself. It is important not to have same on same. If you have people leading a change who previously led an unsuccessful change effort, people will expect failure again if you don't do things differently.

Often structures are over-resourced. It is important to **keep as lean** as possible. The more hierarchical and bureaucratic the team is, the less likely it is that it will be able to execute sustainable change. Lots of people doesn't mean lots of change. The fewer people you need to manage, the less chance there is for communication error or discontent.

ENCOURAGE YOUR 'INTREPRENEURS'

Entrepreneurs are the modern-day business rock stars. They are leading the innovation and disruption charge. They have skill sets that are adaptable, resourceful, creative, collaborative, value-focused and purpose-driven. These are exactly the skills required to survive, adapt and thrive in a disruptive environment. An 'intrepreneur' is somebody who acts like an entrepreneur, but within an organisation. It is very likely that you already have intrepreneurs within your organisation – they have all the skills and the mindset; they just haven't had the environment, culture or support to allow them to shine.

Many organisations talk up the fact they are innovative or have developed innovation capability. But running a one-off hackathon, creating an innovation hub or holding a design-thinking workshop does not make an organisation innovative. What drives innovation is culture, and at the heart of culture are people. An entrepreneurial skillset and mindset needs to be introduced in your organisation so that it can permeate through the whole company. Having intrepreneurs will accelerate this process.

Let's look at some of the ways an intrepreneur could potentially operate in your organisation:

- Identify and facilitate identification of growth opportunities;
- Develop internal capability by facilitating and overseeing a training program on entrepreneurship;

- Develop and continually improve innovation frameworks and methodologies used in the organisation to develop innovation capability;
- Build innovation hubs and centres of learning;
- Collaborate with industry partners, universities, government and other entities to develop innovation; and
- Build an innovation funding model, which may include organisational self-funding, government grants, joint ventures, capital raising or debt.

Remember, however, that an intrepreneur must deliver value. They are not there simply so that an organisation can say that it is 'doing innovation'. Value can be the commercialisation of an innovation, lessons learned from an initiative, or the progression and development of an 'entrepreneurial' culture.

EMBRACE YOUR MISFITS

'Here's to the crazy ones. The misfits. The rebels. The troublemakers. The round pegs in the square holes. The ones who see things differently. They're not fond of rules, and they have no respect for the status quo. You can quote them, disagree with them, glorify and vilify them. About the only thing you can't do is ignore them because they change things. They push humanity forward. And while some may see them as crazy, we see genius. Because the people who are crazy enough to think they can change the world are the ones who do.'

STEVE JOBS

Some of the most important people in your team may be the misfits. But why are they important? Because they bring different

195

perspectives, they bring new ideas, they challenge the status quo and they ask questions that matter. It is of no use to anybody to be surrounded by 'yes' people – people who will just agree with everything you say and allow you to send a space shuttle into flight despite knowing the mission is doomed. This is what happened when the space shuttle Challenger exploded a few seconds after take-off in 1986. Organisational culture and decision-making processes were considered major contributing factors to this disaster, particularly the issue of groupthink, in which irrational decision making was allowed to occur to preserve harmony and conformity.

You don't want 'yes' people, but many managers fall into the trap of employing people with the same style and opinion, or abilities, as their own. Often they employ people who are 'safe', who won't 'rock the boat'. But what you need is diversity and people who will tell a constructive truth. Yes, absolutely, they should be aligned at a values level – that should be non-negotiable – but after that you should be developing a team that can contribute to getting great results, not just compliance and agreement.

Ultimately, you should let the market decide if they are crazy, or if they can solve problems in a meaningful and cost-effective way. Save your judgement, protect these people from the judgement of others, and allow them to do their best work. Help them push their ideas forward and protect them from people who expect everyone to just comply. I could rattle off names like Steve Jobs, Elon Musk, Richard Branson, Jack Ma, Jeff Bezos – they were all misfits, and because they did not conform, they were able to produce brilliance.

TAILOR YOUR TEAM

Albert Einstein wrote, *'Everybody is a genius. But if you judge a fish by its ability to climb a tree, it will live its whole life believing that it is stupid.'*

You need to make sure you have the right people in the right roles. You must match the task to the skill set. People who are asked to perform tasks outside their ability can be become disengaged and disruptive. Sometimes people can simply become bored and need to be repositioned and placed in an environment where they can flourish.

Some people will need to transition to mentoring roles or leadership roles. Others will need to receive more mentoring or should be allowed to focus on something that they excel at, assuming that it is in the team's interests. Some people will need to be right in the action, while others will need to be out of the limelight. It will depend on the game day, and what is needed at the time to achieve your goals. Just don't make your fish climb trees.

EMPLOY PEOPLE WHO CARE

Success is often about positioning and diversity, but it's also about teamwork. Remember that sometimes a team is greater than the sum of the individuals who make it up. Have you ever wondered why sports teams with members who lack skills can be so successful, or, conversely, why a team full of talent doesn't seem to be able to reach its potential? Successful teams pull together for a common goal; unsuccessful teams are full of individuals who put their own interests ahead of those of the team. Your change teams are no different.

People who genuinely do not care will destroy the fabric of your business; they will almost certainly ensure that you do not meet your strategic objectives. They will undermine every move you make, as they are determined to be unhappy and want to ensure that everyone else lives in the same misery. They will influence and infect other people in your organisation, and no one wants to come to work to listen to some negative person complain a lot and contribute little.

As in any great team, if someone is not contributing and will not make the team's goals the priority, then, of course, they should be moved.

If someone really doesn't care about you and your organisation, you can't force them to love what they do, respect your organisation and the people within it, treat the money as if it were their own or put in a meaningful day's effort. What you can do, however, is ensure that you have people in your organisation who have a care factor and who will live by their purpose and values.

We encourage our children to play with other children who are good influences. It's the same at work. How often do we get surrounded by people who just don't care, and who burn our own energy? How demoralising is it when you work hard, but see someone else contributing little yet still pulling a reward? Surround yourself with positive influence, just as you would do for your children.

Energy is contagious – good energy will create more good energy; negative energy will create more negative energy. You need people who can swim in the same direction, people who want to achieve the same outcome and who understand their place in the team and their role in achieving that outcome.

STOP ARGUING ABOUT IT AND START DRIVING THE BUS

While you want the best team you can possibly have, don't make the mistake of trying to perfect it. Humans are, well, human. You can't control your team the way you might be able to control the manufacture of a product. If you're having problems, there may be a point where you just need to move on and show some leadership. You won't be able to please everyone.

For all the planning you do around engagement, empowering, training and communication – there will be times that leadership simply needs to make a call and set the direction. This may make you unpopular. But leadership is not about being popular; it is about doing what is right and leading towards the objective.

The bus must leave at the right time, and it needs the right people on board. Sometimes passengers will miss the stop, and sometimes there won't be enough room to take everyone, but the leader is the driver who decides whether to wait for latecomers, squeeze extra passengers in or just keep driving...

> The fifth step in creating a Change-ready organisation is to build an effective change team.

Change takes effort – it requires leadership, management, governance, administration and resources. The organisation needs to be set up for success, as do those individuals and teams who deliver the change.

Having the organisation change-ready will not only help individual change effort, it will also create a capability in the organisation to make change the norm.

WHAT YOU CAN DO

- ☑ Identify people who will make this happen;
- ☑ Align a senior executive with your change initiative and ensure that they are accountable not only for delivering the initiative, but also for supporting the initiative. Ensure that the senior executive is an advocate of the change;
- ☑ Encourage your 'intrepreneurs' and develop an entrepreneurial capability;
- ☑ Respect and listen to the mavericks, misfits and unconventional members of the organisation; and
- ☑ Review your organisational structure and put the right people in the right roles.

THE PRIZES OF EMBRACING
AND DELIVERING CHANGE

The following embody the benefits of getting this attribute right:

An adaptable organisation

Building change capability into your organisation means that you will become adaptable and be able to respond to market changes as they occur. The organisation will be change-ready and have the necessary skills to be able to deal with any situation, whenever and however it arises. Your organisation will be comfortable with the uncomfortable and embrace uncertainty as an opportunity.

Energy through momentum

As you deliver change, it builds momentum and thirst for more success. This becomes a collective movement, which creates an addiction to delivering impactful change. Confidence will grow and people will start to become bolder, be more willing to share ideas and become more creative. An energy is created around customers and other people and they keep building the energy as they attract more of the same.

A fresh and contemporary organisation

Being able to deliver change means that your organisation will remain relevant. It will be fresh and contemporary, a fun place to work and a great organisation to do business with. The organisation will be creative, using modern tools and methods to solve old and new problems alike. This fresh, fun, energetic mood will be infectious.

Aspirations achieved

One of the most satisfying aspects of being able to deliver change is that you can see your dreams through. Making it happen is very different from talking about it. Knowing that you can make it happen gives you greater confidence to then go on and make more happen, or make bigger things happen. When the organisation can achieve its vision, more opportunities can be created, and more space can be provided to be able to have more impact.

Play on your terms

Delivering change puts the current environment on your terms. You get to call the shots and shape the future. If you are unable to effect change, the environment will start dictating what you must do and how you must do it. Being able to effect change will make you the master of your own destiny and allow you to set the agenda.

LET'S WRAP A BOW AROUND IT AND GET ON WITH IT

GET STARTED

Getting on with it is a recurring theme and message in this book. You need to start creating momentum and energy around what it is that you are trying to do. The simple act of starting builds confidence and trust. People are more likely to get motivated by action than by talk.

As you start you will begin to learn, and one of the things you will learn early is where to focus and bring your energy. You will be surprised at how quickly this happens. You will also be surprised at how many people will want to help and build the energy with you. Your energy will be contagious.

KEEP IT SIMPLE

As you go about your innovation journey and set your organisation up for lasting success, make sure you keep it simple. Innovation does not have to be about coming up with a brilliant invention that will change all of humanity. Remember that people just want solutions to their problems, and the simpler the solution is, the more likely it is that it will be adopted and sustained. Most importantly, there is value in simplicity.

A great deal of energy and resource can be wasted on trying to come up with the best, most sophisticated solution when that is not what is required. We must remember that this is never about us; it is about the people we are creating value for, and those people are our customers. The customer does not have the bandwidth to consume all the stimuli that this world offers, so you need to be doing them a favour and making things simple. Simple is also fast. The simpler it is, the easier it is for people to understand, test, adopt and provide feedback.

GET HELP

You cannot do this alone. Seek out the support you need in the places that you need it most. Many hands make light work, and sometimes you or the organisation itself will not have all the answers or competencies. Get help while you build that capability.

We are always learning, and we can accelerate that process by working with the people who already understand it and know what it is like to have walked in your shoes. Look inside your organisation for people who have done this before. Seek the help of consultants in the short term while you build internal capability. Ask for help from industry associations or governments, who have a plethora of resources available. You might also be able to work with some smaller perhaps disruptive firms that can help you on your journey and accelerate both your growth aspirations and theirs.

When you do get help, make sure that you don't just get someone in to tell you what you already know. The help you really need will lift the capability of your organisation and allow it to become self-sufficient. Don't give the organisation a fish; teach it to fish.

EAT THE ELEPHANT

How do you eat an elephant? One bite at a time.

Organisations are not easy to operate at the best of times. Overlaying a critical need to adapt to disruptive and uncertain environments can make the task of steering them seem insurmountable.

But you don't have to eat all the elephant at once. All you need to do is to get very clear on how you will approach your change initiative and get started. Lots of little efforts will ultimately make up a big effort.

Think about it this way: If you have every single person in your organisation focused on doing one small thing that contributes to your big picture, I think you will find there will be a massive shift. If everybody takes a small bite, it won't take long to eat the elephant.

THINK OF THE FUTURE

Your efforts need to be sustainable. Not only do the people who are working hard on the change deserve to see the fruits of their efforts, the whole purpose and intention of the change is to ensure your relevance as an organisation. If the change does not stick, you will not be relevant.

Transformations of scale are most certainly not set-and-forgets. They must be an infinite loop. There need to be strong systems in place so that the transformation can be replicated – day in and day out. And not just for one initiative, but for the continuous cycle of solving meaningful problems by providing value-adding solutions. It must become part of the organisation's DNA.

It is not to say there won't be wobbles. There will be. It is also not to say that everything will be a success. These matters are never a straight line; rather, they are a squiggle that goes around and around, darts forward, falls back, does a few loops and sometimes changes course. Being comfortable with this ambiguity is important. It is about everyone in your organisation being able to see the bigger picture and giving them the resilience to keep pushing ahead. Don't let people get spooked and cry that the whole effort is in vain when one small thing falls over. Strong, calm and communicative leadership is required.

Change is a continuum; you can never be complacent. You may initiate and implement change today, but things will continue to change around you, and not only do you need to be ready, but you need to be actively changing to remain relevant.

The Fit for Disruption model deliberately spends a lot of time focusing on culture and mindset. With a strong culture and an optimistic mindset, the chances of sustaining the effort will be exponential. Ultimately, if your people are empowered and driving the effort, in line with strategic objectives, the likelihood of sustainability will be high. Or let's go the other way; if you do not have the people on board, you will not get the result you want.

Leaders should build into their daily work practices time to ensure that sustainability is achieved. This may be as simple as taking a walk through the teams, having discussions with your customers or building relationships with the teams who are closest to delivering the outcome.

This is also why having strong commercial disciplines is important when it comes to delivering transformative and disruptive innovation. The disciplines will enable the change to be measured, and also provide the frameworks to ensure that it is done properly and executed appropriately. The commercial focus is about bringing visibility not just to the process, but also the result – the benefits that will be derived.

Finally, to be sustainable, the change needs to be profitable. Value must be created. It needs to provide a return greater than the alternative. These are basic business principles, but they are often forgotten, and many transformative efforts have failed because they failed to focus on tangible results.

CELEBRATE

You and your people will experience many emotions as you all place a great deal of effort, energy and commitment into change. There will be times that you are frustrated, times that you wonder whether it will ever fall into place. But it will.

As you start to get some wins on the board, celebrate. Celebrate the small wins, the big wins. Acknowledge efforts and recognise contribution. Every step of the way. Do not wait until the end – that will be too late. In fact, the end never arrives because we want to build a business where change is a capability, not an event.

Work should be a fun place to be and it should fill us with a sense of purpose. It is important to be reminded of that and not take things so seriously all the time.

Success breeds success, so why not celebrate it every chance you get? It will only help the innovative process.

REMEMBER THAT LEADERSHIP IS A PRIVILEGE

Business is in the wonderful position of being able to impact the lives of many. We have an opportunity now to shape the world and build opportunities for everyone. While the world is not such a bad place, despite what all the news tells us, we still have a long way to go.

Through your ability to innovate, you will have an opportunity to make a positive difference, and that should not be undervalued. You will have the opportunity to improve the lives of many.

Every contribution will help, no matter how big or small, as long as we all swim in the same direction – making our world a better place.

Good luck, have fun, continue to dream big and, most importantly, make those dreams become a reality.

ABOUT THE AUTHOR

Matthew brings over twenty years international experience leading finance and commercial functions, large-scale operations and transformation programs. He has worked across the globe with organisations undergoing immense change, developing and applying the principles of the Fit for Disruption model.

He is now an innovation and business transformation author and speaker, and founder of the Menark Group – a specialist strategy, program delivery and training organisation that focuses on driving business performance by developing commercial, operational and innovation capability.

Matthew holds a Bachelor of Business (Accounting) from Monash University, and has completed the Stanford LEAD program in Corporate Innovation.

Matthew wrote *Fit for Disruption* not only to help leaders and emerging leaders develop the capability to manage disruption, but also to inspire a new brand of leadership that can make this world a better place. At the heart of this ambition is the belief that businesses can, and must, drive positive social and economic value, and improve the lives and wellbeing of the communities in which they operate.

Matthew also loves to help people develop and reach their full potential. He believes the greatest waste of all is the waste of human potential, but that business can harness this potential and create an environment where people can be the very best versions of themselves. Matthew believes that environments that do not support the growth of the people and communities they serve are only adding to the epidemic of mental health issues, family breakdown and economic suffering. Matthew wants to help reverse this trend, and believes that this starts with the will of our business leaders to create environments that foster the development of human potential.

Please connect with Matthew on

in www.linkedin.com/in/matthewcwebber

✉ or drop him a note at m.webber@menark.com.au.

ABOUT THE MENARK GROUP

The Menark Group builds business improvement and training programs that transform the culture and profitability of organisations – it makes them Fit for Disruption.

The Group is focused on supporting leaders, and emerging leaders, to build the capability to deal with a disruptive environment, while also providing insights, tools and support that will help businesses transform and thrive in times of rapid change.

Menark offers expert facilitation, training, strategic planning and program delivery services for organisations that wish to improve business performance, develop innovation as a core organisational strength, and transform their businesses – profitably. Menark delivers profitable results through customised programs that focus on:

- Training and Development;
- Business Design and Cost Transformation;
- Commercial and Supply Chain Optimisation; and
- Program and Change Management.

The Menark Group transforms with profitable impact and builds enduring capability.

To help leaders and emerging leaders, a range of resources have been developed and are available from the Menark website, along with links to other useful resources. These include articles, insights, tips, templates, guides and tools, which are updated regularly.

Keep in touch at:

🌐 www.menark.com.au

✉ m.webber@menark.com.au

www.ingramcontent.com/pod-product-compliance
Lightning Source LLC
Chambersburg PA
CBHW071557210326
41597CB00019B/3285